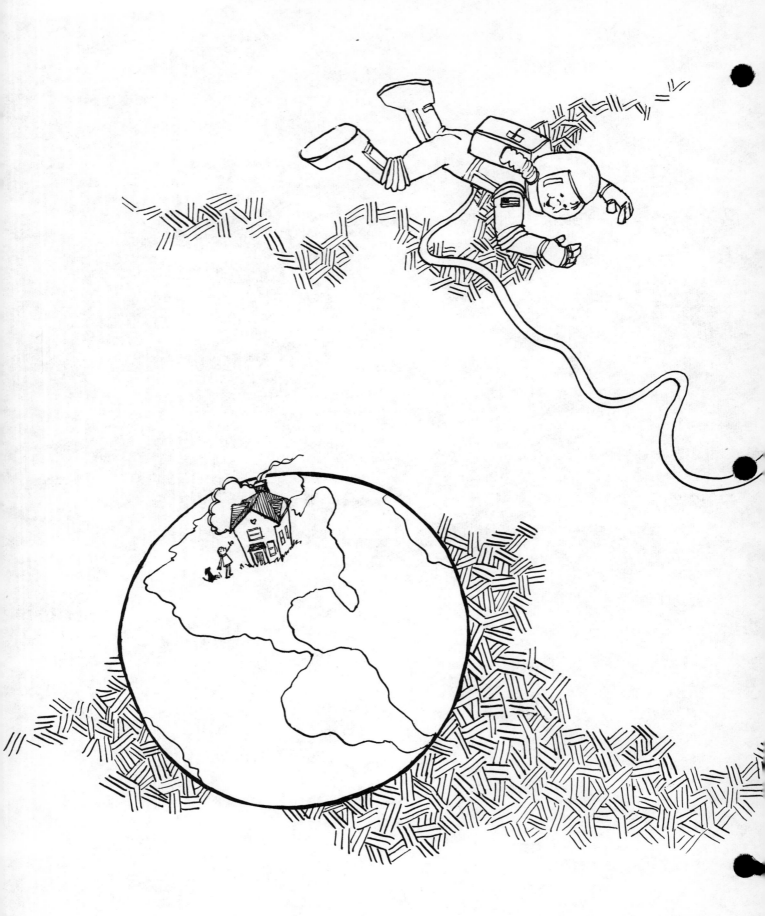

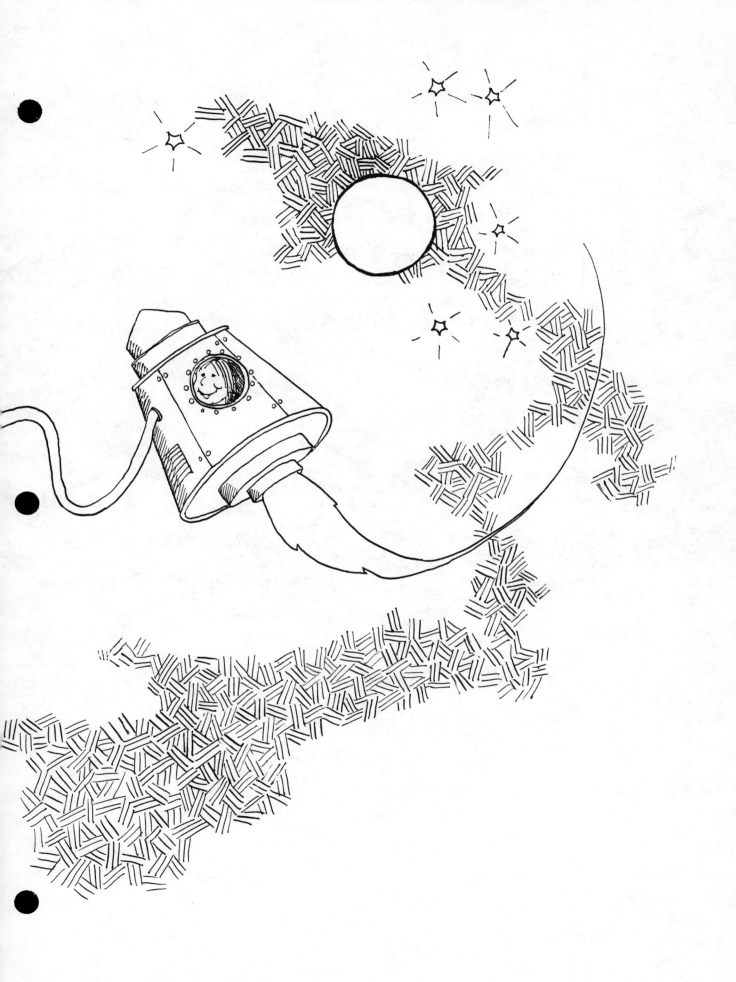

# Kids' Stuff SOCIAL STUDIES

BY IMOGENE FORTE
AND JOY MAC KENZIE

illustrated by Gayle Seaberg

Library of Congress Card Number 76-20952
ISBN 0-913916-23-4

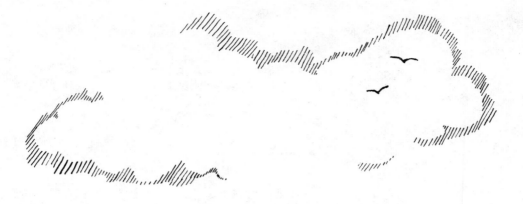

To Shana and Kristen..

Two beautiful little girls whose lives
touch ours in special ways that afford
glimpses into the magic world of
childhood and beyond.

# PREFACE

As boys and girls grow and develop awareness they innately seek their own places as persons of worth and dignity, unique in their own rights. Television, radio, books, magazines, and family travel enable the average child of today to acquire broader social horizons by the time he enters the middle grades than his great-grandparents may have reached in a lifetime of study and observation. Teachers and parents then are faced with the awesome challenge of helping these youngsters sort out and make meaningful use of the concepts and skills necessary for positive interaction with their peers and for expanding social horizons to include people, places, and events beyond their own immediate environment. It is in response to this need that Kids' Stuff Social Studies has been written.

The authors' goal for a balanced social studies program for the elementary school is to help boys and girls understand and accept themselves and others and to function effectively as responsible citizens within the context of the world in which they live. The activities presented here have been designed to be compatible with and incorporated into the framework of established social studies programs. Their purpose is to provide motivation, reinforcement, and enrichment for ongoing concept development and skills usage. An attempt has been made to render them adaptable to the unique needs of teachers and students in either self-contained classrooms or open school settings. In most instances they can be adjusted for use with large or small groups. Some activities will be especially effective when presented on an individual basis as independent study, diagnostic and prescriptive programs, in a student tutorial plan, or in learning centers.

The activities have been sequentially categorized into three major areas: Close to Home, Outward Bound, and The World and Beyond. There is nothing sacred about the order or manner of their presentation or the individual plans for classroom implementation. Each activity includes a specific purpose and step-by-step procedures for classroom use. All activities are non-rigidly structured and many of them include suggested extensions or adaptations to promote flexibility in presentation.

The very practical appendix includes additional plans, a creative sociogram, a unique individual reading record, study outlines, student and teacher references, and a complete social studies check list to assess pupil growth.

Once again, some of the ideas presented here are brand new, some of them are oldies but goodies, and some of them are old ideas with a new twist. There's just one thing they all have in common. The authors are excited about them and would like to try any one of them in an elementary classroom with real live boys and girls next Monday morning. With pride and humility we ask you to be our guest. Choose and use the parts of the book that make sense to you and have fun as you teach and learn about the world and beyond.

Imogene Forte
Joy MacKenzie

# TABLE OF CONTENTS

IV.    APPENDIX

CLOSE
TO HOME

*notes* . . . .

## AS YOU LIKE IT

Purpose: After completing this activity the student should be able to display increased understanding of the influence of classroom environment on student attitudes and behavior.

1.   Discuss different approaches to classroom arrangement and organization in a total group setting. Encourage the students to be free and open in their appraisal of this classroom setting and of other classroom environments they have known. Try to direct the discussion to highlight strengths and weaknesses of each of the arrangements presented and to promote student objectivity.

2.   Ask questions such as:

(1)   How much freedom of movement do you feel is helpful to learning?

(2)   Do you think students should be able to sit anywhere they wish and to change seats as often as they wish?

(3)   Would you like to be completely free to study any one thing you choose for as long as you like without having to put an unfinished project away to move on to the next one? If your answer is yes, do you think this could be worked out to be practical in your classroom? If so, how?

(4)   Can you think of a better way to make art supplies and instructional materials freely available to students?

(5)   What do the terms "open education" and "traditional education" mean to you? Which type of education do you think is best?

3.  Ask the students to work in small groups to plan the classroom as they would like it to be. Provide large sheets of poster paper and instruct each group to graphically portray the desired arrangement for furniture, books, and equipment.

4.  Reassemble the large group and provide time for one spokesman from each small group to present the plan formulated by that group and to respond to questions and concerns related to the plan.

5.  Culminate the discussion with an election to select the best plan for the classroom. Ask the students in the elected group to plan to arrive early the next morning to rearrange the furniture, supplies, and equipment to correspond to their plan.

6.  Allow the class to spend the entire school day in the classroom environment provided by the elected group. At the end of the day launch a discussion to evaluate the effectiveness of the new arrangement. Direct questions to focus on behavior changes, student attitudes, opportunities for group interaction, availability of needed supplies, and overall physical comfort.

7.  Encourage the students to select parts of the plan that "really work" and that they would like to keep, suggest modifications, and to assist in rearranging the facilities for the                next day.

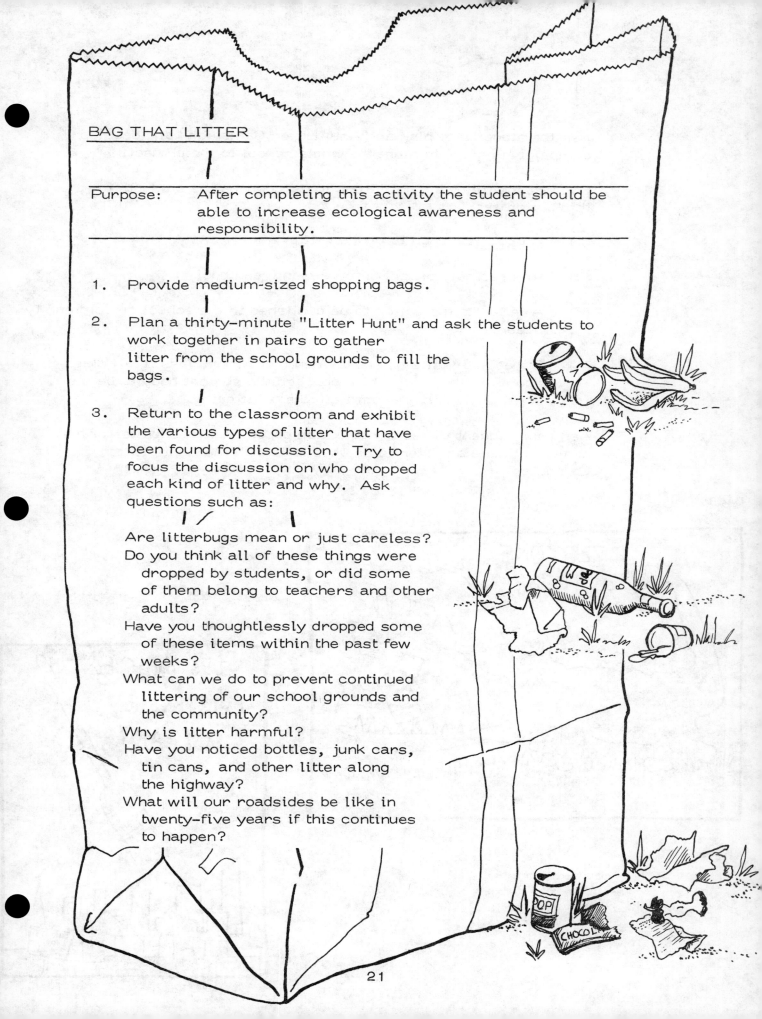

## BAG THAT LITTER

**Purpose:** After completing this activity the student should be able to increase ecological awareness and responsibility.

1. Provide medium-sized shopping bags.

2. Plan a thirty-minute "Litter Hunt" and ask the students to work together in pairs to gather litter from the school grounds to fill the bags.

3. Return to the classroom and exhibit the various types of litter that have been found for discussion. Try to focus the discussion on who dropped each kind of litter and why. Ask questions such as:

   Are litterbugs mean or just careless?
   Do you think all of these things were dropped by students, or did some of them belong to teachers and other adults?
   Have you thoughtlessly dropped some of these items within the past few weeks?
   What can we do to prevent continued littering of our school grounds and the community?
   Why is litter harmful?
   Have you noticed bottles, junk cars, tin cans, and other litter along the highway?
   What will our roadsides be like in twenty-five years if this continues to happen?

21

4.  Ask the students to plan an "Anti-Litter Campaign" and develop campaign strategy to alert the whole school to the project.

    Suggest the following activities and encourage the students to think of others:

    (1)  A protest march to protest litterers.

    (2)  An assembly program for the entire school.

    (3)  A letter to the editor to be published in the school or community paper.

    (4)  Scheduled visits by spokesmen from your class to all class-rooms in the school to encourage the student body to be more conscious of the harmful effects of littering.

5.  Ask each student to use construction paper and art supplies of his choice to make a poster to be used to launch the "Anti-Litter Campaign".

# BOX TOWN, U. S. A.

**Purpose:** After completing this activity the student should be able to increase his awareness of the make-up of the immediate community.

1. Provide a collection of cereal boxes of various shapes and sizes, tempera paint, construction paper, felt tip pens, crayons, paste, scissors, and an old bed sheet.

2. Talk with students in a group setting about the community in which they live. Lead the discussion to draw on student aware- ness of buildings, streets, vacant lots, parks and/or features unique to the community.

3. Plan and conduct a class field trip to observe the actual make-up of the community. Ask the students to make notes to help in constructing a model of the community.

4. Return to the classroom to construct the model community. Ask the students to assist in drawing in outline form the streets and/or roads that comprise the community as they have just viewed it. The plan may be first drawn on the chalk board and then transferred to a large bed sheet placed on the floor.

5. Direct the students to work individually, in pairs, or in small groups to make buildings from the cereal boxes and art supplies.

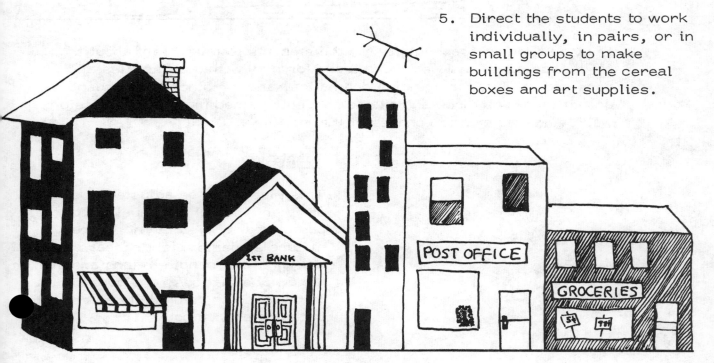

6.  Place the cereal boxes in appropriate spots on the streets and roads drawn on the bed sheet.

7.  Make traffic lights, street signs, trees, flowers, grass, and billboards from various art supplies to add realistic interest to the model.

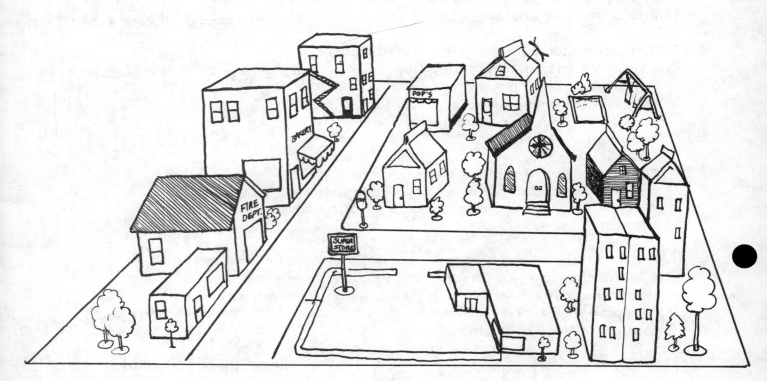

8.  Provide time and opportunity for the students to talk freely about the model community. Use it as a focus for play with doll families and cars and trucks, for creative dramatics, and for other independent activities to reinforce and extend concepts gained from the discussion, walk, and construction phases of this activity.

Adaptation:

This plan could be adjusted to studies of other types of communities of the past, a park, or a farm. More mature students might research the way of life of people in long ago and/or far away situations, and construct a model of their community as reflected in the reference books.

## BRIDGING THE GENERATION GAP

Purpose:     After completing this center the student should be able to empathize with people of different ages.

1.    Provide a variety of resource books, magazines, paste, a hat box, scissors, and 4 x 6" index cards.

2.    Talk with the students about their day-to-day life at school and at home.  Direct attention to clothes, food, transportation, recreation, and other common aspects of daily life.  Read and discuss concepts of how people in times past lived and compare and contrast daily life today with daily life in the past.

3.    Instruct each student to develop at least three questions they would like to ask someone ten years older than they are, someone twenty years older, and someone fifty years older.  Ask them to print the questions on 4 x 6" index cards.

4.    Collect all the cards to be placed in the "Bridge the Generation Gap" box.  The students may assist in making the box by looking in the magazines for pictures of people of all ages involved in many different activities.  Ask each student to select one picture to cut out and paste (collage fashion) on a large hat box.  Cut a hole in the top of the box to form a slot.

5. Invite resource people in each of the age brackets to come to the classroom to answer questions to be drawn from the box. Tape record the question-and-answer sessions.

6. Arrange time after the last resource person's visit for the students to listen to the tapes in chronological order. Lead a culminating discussion of differences observed in each of the ten-year periods and of the implications of these differences on the development of thought and life styles.

Adaptation:

Younger and less mature students might profit from a simpler approach to this activity. They might develop fewer and less complex questions to be written on a chart and used in interviews with two or three people representative of different age ranges. The taping activities would be omitted.

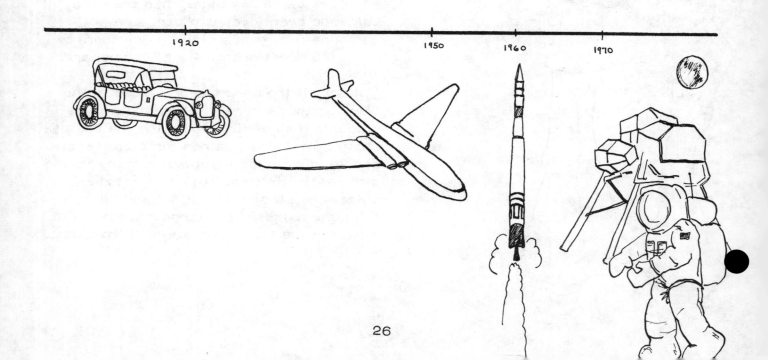

BROOK-LOOK

Purpose:    After completing this activity the student should be
            able to demonstrate his understanding of the origin and
            characteristics of a brook.

1.    Provide all available resource materials on brooks and brook life
      (see Bibliography).  If possible read Margaret Farnington Bartlett's
      Where The Brook Begins or The Clean Brook aloud to the students.

2.    Ask the students to listen carefully or to read for themselves to find
      answers to the following questions:

      (1)    Where does the water in a brook come from?
             (rain, melted snow and ice, springs, ponds, swamps)

      (2)    How does a little brook become a big brook?
             (little paths of water join together to make big ones)

      (3)    What kinds of things do you find in a brook?
             (sticks, stones, pebbles, grass, soil, sand, twigs,
             seeds, leaves, etc.)

      (4)    What kinds of animals are found in or near a brook?
             How does each use the brook?
             (small animals, i.e., squirrels, chipmunks, deer, rabbits,
             beaver, raccoons, skunks, frogs, snakes, insects and spiders,
             fish, snails, crabs, lizards, etc.)

      (5)    Where do brooks go?
             (to ponds, rivers, and lakes, etc.)

      (6)    Why does the earth need brooks?
             (to carry melted snow and ice away so it won't flood the land.)

      (7)    How do brooks help people?
             (to provide water and homes for animals)

      (8)    How can people help brooks?
             (by keeping them clean)

3.    Reproduce the following pupil activity page--one for each student--or
      create a copy large enough for the entire group of students to use.

4. Ask students to fill in the brook scene by adding all the kinds of things found in and near a brook.

Adaptation:

Create a sandbox brook scene or use an aluminum foil brook packed in soil in a long flower box to make a more realistic "brook".

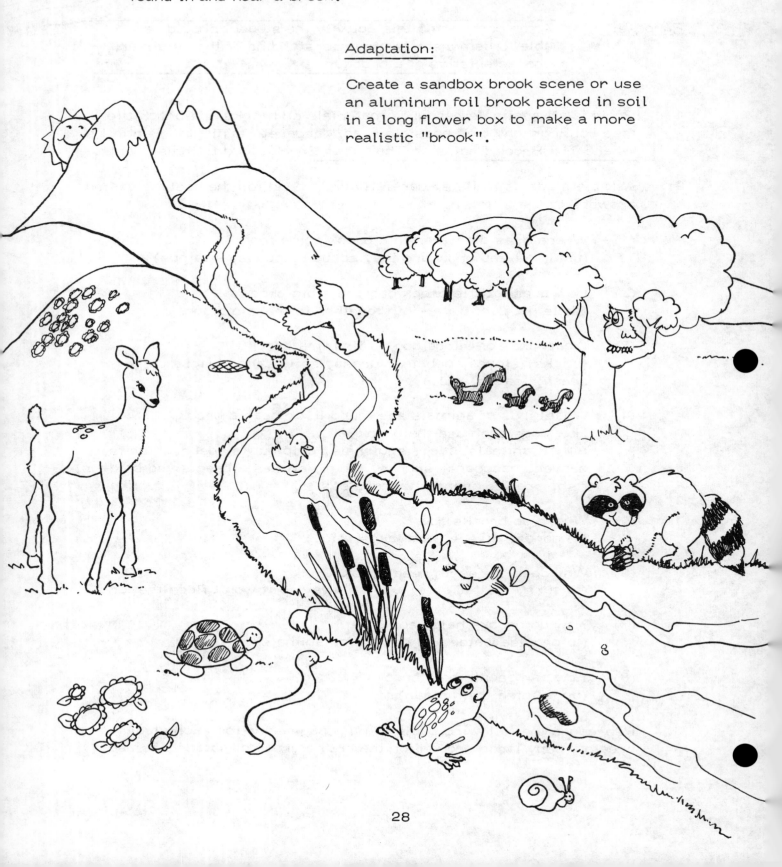

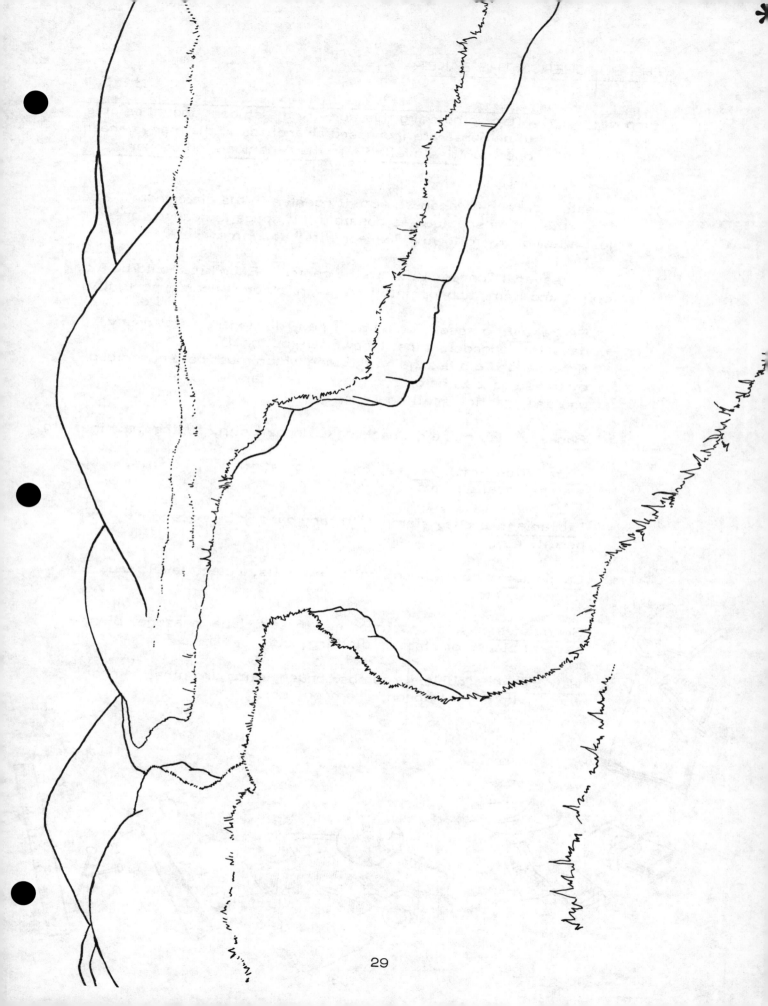

Purpose:   After completing this activity the student should be able to demonstrate increased awareness of the many career opportunities available to the American job seeker.

1.   Create a career-awareness activity center in the classroom. Keep it simple but as spacious as possible. If space is scarce, present just a few of the following "career kits" at a time.

2.   Place several "career kits" in the center. Each kit should be a box containing items appropriate to a given job or career opportunity.

Secretary: glasses, steno pad, pen, dictionary, stationery, cassette recorder, tape, typewriter (optional).
(Pre-record a message on the tape which must be transcribed by the student as he or she plays "secretary". Great way to use and practice spelling words!)

Banker: play money, checkbook, deposit slip, adding machine, etc.

Post Office Employee: stamps, letters, money, pencils, rubber stamps, scales, etc.

Librarian: books, stamps, library cards, index card file box, pencil, etc.

Carpenter: tools, wood, nails, overalls, ruler, level, tape measure, etc.

Seamstress: scissors, needles, thread, tape measure, pins, several pieces of cloth or clothing, etc.

Hairdresser: curlers, combs, brush, clips and pins, mirror, wigs, hair dryer, apron, shampoo, etc.

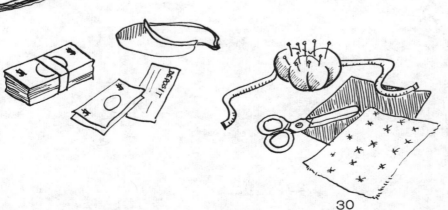

3. Ask students to visit the center several times and experiment with the kits. (Instructions may accompany kits as needed.)

4. Have books, films, slides, tapes, posters, etc. related to career opportunities as a part of the center decor and optional activity.

5. Use a sharing time as a culminating activity for summarizing and reinforcing awareness, student discoveries, and reactions. (Perhaps each student might identify the career kit he most enjoyed using and tell why.)

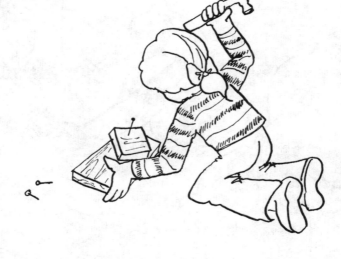

# A CHILD FOR ALL SEASONS

Purpose: After completing this activity the student should be able to name the four seasons and select clothing appropriate for each season.

1. Use a time line or calendar to name the months in each season and discuss the names winter, spring, summer, and fall. Talk about the kind of weather common to each season.

2. Discuss other areas of the country where the seasons may be quite different.

3. Introduce Sally Spring, Willie Winter, Susan Summer, and Fred Fall.

4. Give each child a copy of the dolls and the clothing pages. Ask them to color and cut out clothes and dress each doll appropriately.

Adaptation:

For older or more capable students, groups may be assigned to create a diorama of one of the seasons. Then the dolls may be placed in their appropriate settings.

33

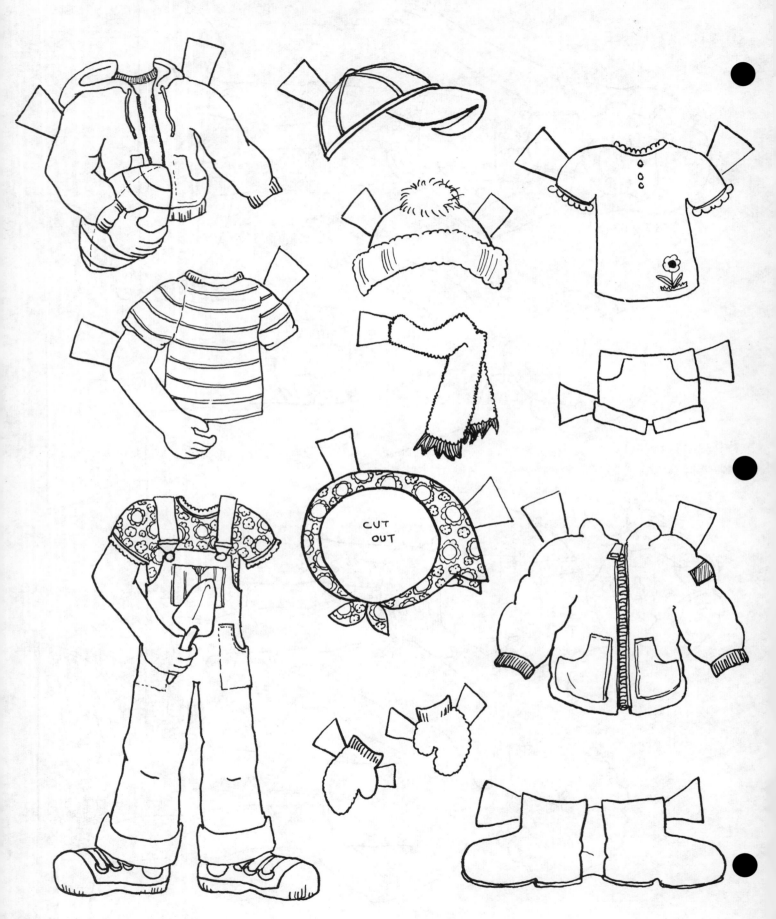

CUT OUT

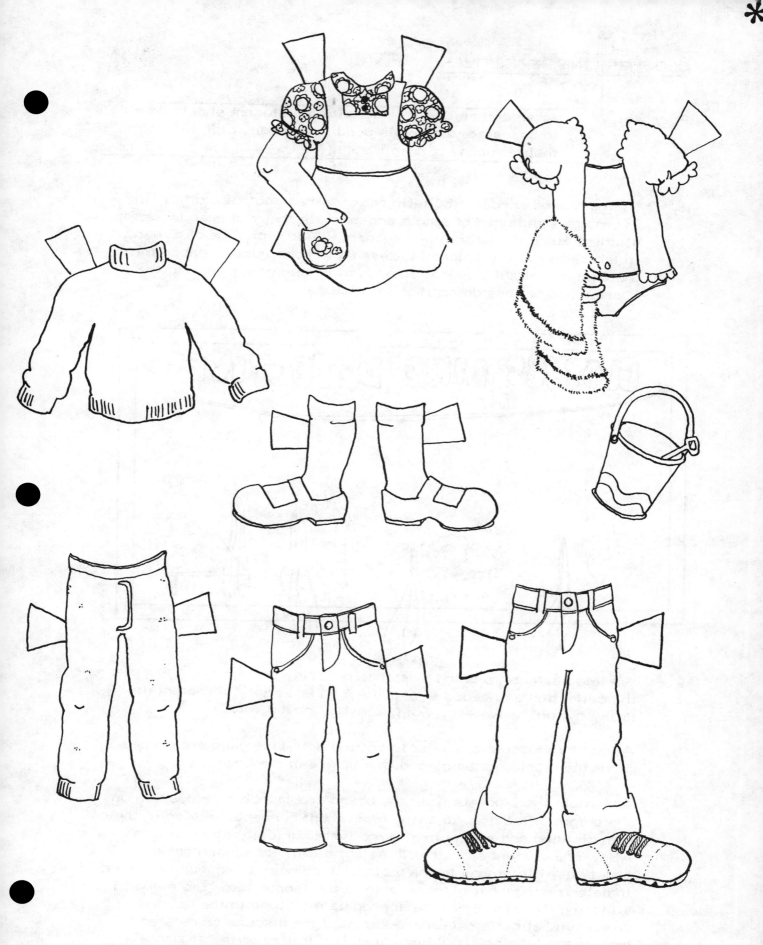

CLOTHES LINE DETECTIVES

Purpose: After completing this activity the student should be able to associate materials used in ordinary clothing with their sources of origin.

1. String a cord across a bulletin board to resemble a clothes line. Thumb tack pictures of plants and animals that are resources for clothing along the bottom of the board. Add a picture of a man in lab setting. Cut colored letters from construction paper for the title and attach several strands of red or green yarn to the board in a spot beside each of the pictures.

2. Ask the students to bring swatches of fabric from home. Supplement the collection as needed to provide a wide variety of materials (silk, cotton, velveteen, wool, plastic, rayon, etc.)

3. Allow the students to assist in cutting doll-size garment shapes from the fabrics to be placed in a box near the board.

4. Assemble the students near the board and launch a discussion on the origin of fabrics, drawing from them concepts related to their own clothing and attempting to motivate curiosity about others. Allow one student at a time to select a miniature garment to "tell about" as it is pinned to the clothes line. Ask the group to assist in determining what plant or animal the fabric came from and in attaching the yarn from the appropriate picture to the fabric. When synthetic materials are selected the discussion related to man-made fabrics should be carefully limited to the students' maturity level and capacity for understanding.

5. Let students paste a variety of small fabric squares to construction paper to make a collage as a follow-up activity. They could take this home to discuss with their parents.

Adaptation:

More mature students would profit from researching the process used to convert raw materials into fabric.

## CULTURE CACHE

Purpose:
After completing this activity the student should be able to select everyday items representative of his understanding of today's culture.

1.   Reproduce a copy of the "Culture Cache" on the following page for each student.

2.   Record the following script on cassette tape:

"Anthropologists and other scientists travel all over the world looking for artifacts left by people who lived many years ago. These artifacts include remnants of clothing, cooking and hunting utensils, weapons, household goods, and many other items. They are found in caves, underground, in rocky cliff caverns, and in other places that have provided protective covering to prevent decay over the years. By studying these items very carefully the scientists have been able to learn a great deal about the life of the people who left them behind. Sometimes whole cultures never before dreamed of have been discovered in this manner.

"Because many people today realize how important this kind of information is, they make the effort to prepare collections to leave behind to tell the story of their particular time and place for the benefit of future generations. These collections are carefully planned to include items that will be reflective of the activities, cultural interests, hopes, and dreams of the person (or group) preparing them. They must be very carefully selected if they are to give a true picture of the culture they represent hundreds of years from now. Naturally only non-perishable items are included and the whole packet must be carefully prepared for long-term storage. Metal boxes are usually used and are placed in a place designated in a written document or in some other manner apt to survive the ages.

"As a civic responsibility and a concern for passing along some of the values and ideas that you feel are reflective of today's culture, you are being asked to select five items to include in a "culture cache" for future generations. Think very carefully about what our world is really like, about the extent of use of each item you select, and about the actual significance of the item to your way of life.

"Since the real items would be hard to prepare and store, we will make graphic illustrations.

"Take one of the "culture cache" sheets from the box and use black felt tip pens to draw pictures of no fewer than three and no more than five items you have selected after very careful thought. (You may wish to draw the items lightly with pencil first, since it is very important for them to be as clearly portrayed as possible.) Label each item. Use the back of the sheet of paper to state briefly and concisely why you selected each item.

"While you work be thinking about where and how the completed "culture caches" should be stored for the future.

"Turn off the tape and begin work!"

3.   Place the "Culture Cache" sheets, cassette recorder with tape, black felt tip pens, pencils, ball point pens, an instruction card, and a box labeled "Completed Culture Caches" in a learning center or independent work activity setting.

4.   Provide motivation for the activity through class discussion or by viewing a film of the life of people living in a long ago and faraway place.

THIS
CULTURE CACHE
BELONGS TO

IT WAS MADE ON

NAME:

DATE:

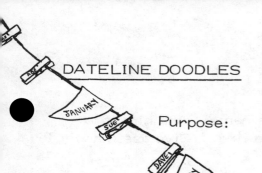

# DATELINE DOODLES

Purpose: After completing this activity the student should be able to demonstrate his understanding of a year as a span of time, divided into twelve segments called months, and identify several important dates or events.

1. String a clothesline the length of the classroom about two feet higher than the students' heads.

2. Divide the clothesline into twelve even segments and label each part with a paper flag or tape tab to denote the twelve months of the year. (This will reinforce the idea of the year as a long expanse of time divided into twelve parts.)

3. Draw or tape pictures on clip-type clothespins that are associated with major United States holidays (i.e., a Santa for Christmas, a menorah for Hanukkah, a rabbit for Easter, a pumpkin for Hallo-ween, a flag or firecracker for the Fourth of July, etc.).

4. Prepare one clothespin bearing the name of each child.

5. Discuss the length of time in a year—365 days—divided into twelve months. Name the months as you touch each part. Then show one of the "holiday" clothespins you have made. Ask students to help you decide in which month it comes and whether near the beginning, middle, or end of the month. Clip it in the appropriate space on the line. Continue likewise with the others you have made.

6.     Give each student the clothespin bearing his name. Ask him to identify his birthday and place the pin on the line. (Give assistance if necessary.)

Adaptation:

Students may be given additional pins on which to doodle a picture or name which represents a date important in their lives. (It may be a national holiday or it may be the day they got a new puppy.)

For older or more capable students, use a similar technique to create historic time lines, chain of events, etc.

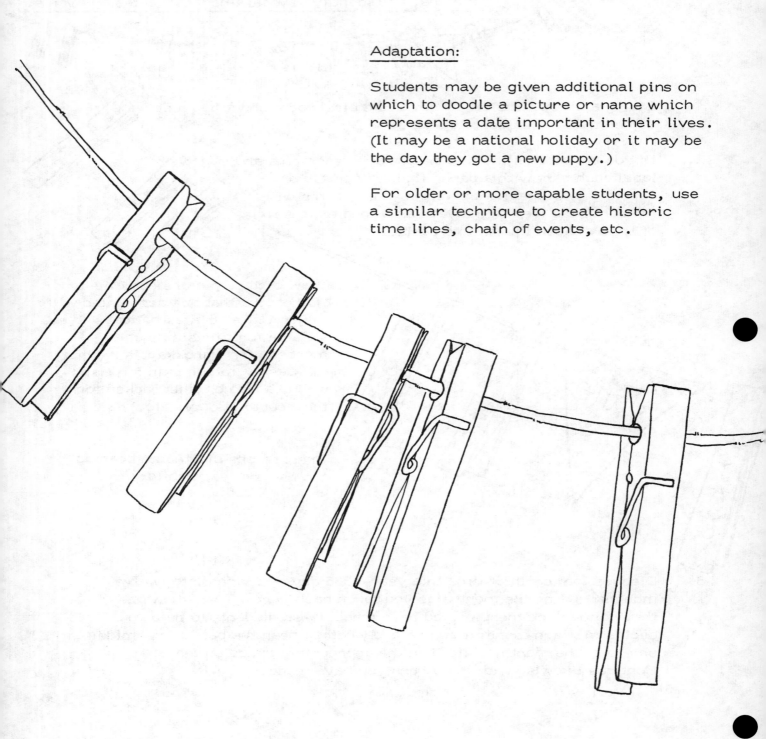

42

# DEAR OLD GOLDEN RULE DAY

Purpose:   After completing this activity the student should be able
to creatively interpret ideas and personal feelings
associated with the school day.

1.   Lead a group discussion of the scheduled activities of the entire
school day.  Ask each student to select one phase of the school
day that they especially enjoy or appreciate.  As the review
continues, list the activities on the chalk board as they are named.

2.   Distribute shirt cardboards (from the laundry) or squares of tagboard,
crayons, scissors, and manila envelopes.

3.   Instruct each student to draw a picture representative of the phase
of the school day he selected as "special" and to cut the picture into
large pieces to make a jigsaw puzzle.

4.   Upon completion the pieces of each jigsaw puzzle should be placed
in a manila envelope and put in a designated area easily accessible
to other students.  The student's name should be written in small
letters on the flap of the envelope.

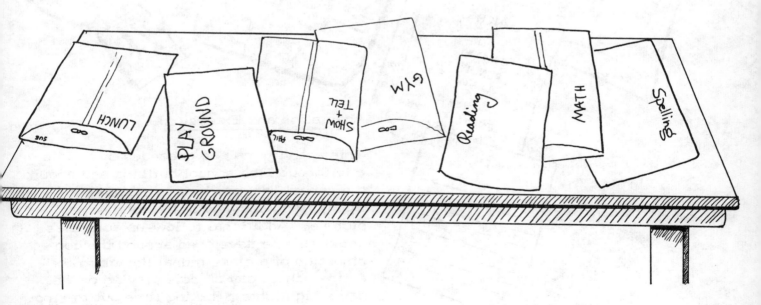

5.   Add sheets of writing paper and pencils to the center.

6.   Have students take one envelope at a time from the center and put
the jigsaw puzzle together to identify the part of the school day
illustrated as a free time activity.

7.    Ask the student to take a sheet of writing paper from the center after he has worked the puzzle and write a story, poem, or opinion paragraph about the subject of the puzzle. He then adds the creative writing sheet to the envelope with the puzzle pieces, writes his name on the outside of the envelope, and returns the envelope to the center for use by other students. As continued use is made of the puzzles and the collection of creative writing grows, each envelope will become increasingly interesting.

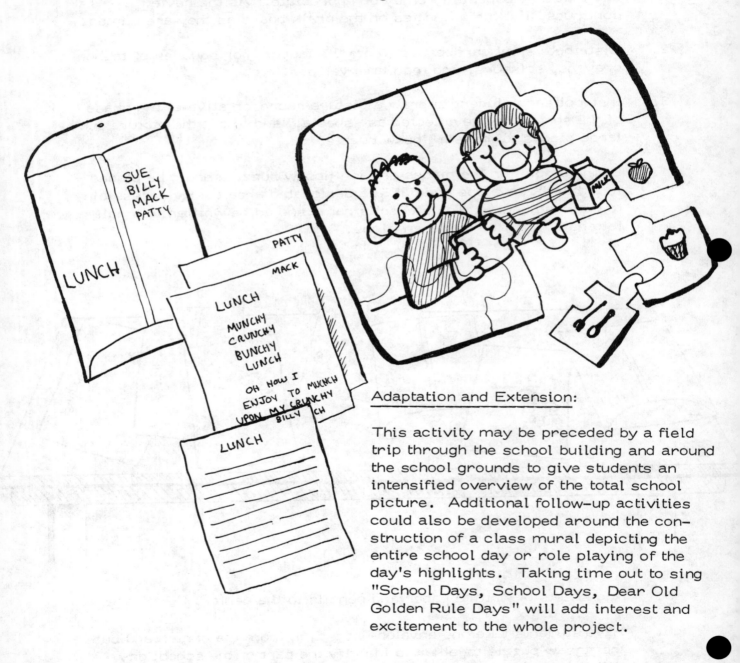

Adaptation and Extension:

This activity may be preceded by a field trip through the school building and around the school grounds to give students an intensified overview of the total school picture. Additional follow-up activities could also be developed around the construction of a class mural depicting the entire school day or role playing of the day's highlights. Taking time out to sing "School Days, School Days, Dear Old Golden Rule Days" will add interest and excitement to the whole project.

44

# DOCTOR, DOCTOR, CAN YOU TELL

Purpose:
After completing this activity the student should be acquainted with the job descriptions of a medical doctor, a dentist, and a pharmacist, and be able to tell how each one helps to keep people healthy.

1. Introduce the three professions of doctor, dentist, and pharmacist by inviting one member of each profession to visit the classroom, bring some of his tools, and tell what he or she does to help keep people healthy. (Note: At least one of these professionals should be a woman!)

   Or arrange a field trip to the doctor's office and drugstore to gain the same information.

   A third choice could be provided by using resource books and pictures and/or borrowing instruments to create a simulated experience.

2. Help children become acquainted with the common tools or instruments used by each of the three professionals.

3. Create a feeling of trust and respect for each one of the professionals by the students.

4. Supply or have students bring a small box or sack which can be used to create a professional kit or bag. (Though pharmacists don't generally carry a bag, they might bring one to class to show some of their equipment, i.e., measuring devices, pill boxes and bottles, prescription pads, etc.)

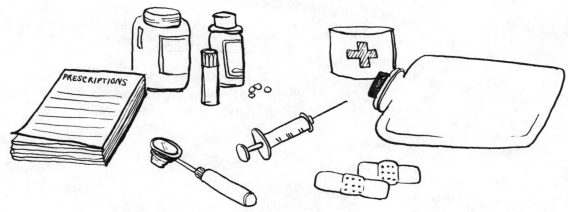

5.  Ask each student to assume the role of a doctor, dentist, or pharmacist and create a "pretend" collection of tools and instruments that person might use to help keep children well.

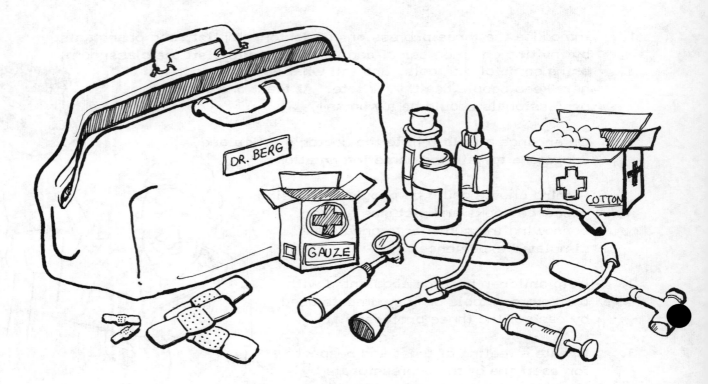

6.  When the "kits" are done, ask each student to introduce himself as Dr. _____, show the contents of his kit, and tell how each item is used; then explain to students how important it is to help keep people well and invite the class to visit his or her office or pharmacy regularly.

Adaptation:

The above procedure may be followed to introduce many other professions.

## DON'T THROW IT AWAY

Purpose: After completing this activity the student should be able to demonstrate creative awareness of secondary uses for recyclable materials.

1. Collect items ordinarily disposed of after initial use but with recycling possibilities. Some easily acquired articles are:

   nylon hose

   styrofoam egg carton

   plastic berry box

   half gallon waxed milk carton

   mesh onion or orange bag

   plastic dry cleaning bag

   wooden cigar box

   styrofoam meat tray

   peanut butter and/or mayonnaise jar

   paper towel or toilet tissue roll

   outgrown skirt

   odds and ends of yarn

   old shower curtain

   plastic detergent bottle

   Sunday newspaper

2. Wrap one object for each student in used gift wrap or tissue paper, brown paper or department store bags, comic or want-ad sections of the newspaper, or in plastic bags from specialty shops. Tie with used gift wrap ribbon, string, or yarn. (Yarn may be acquired by raveling old sweaters.) Assemble all wrapped packages in a bushel fruit basket labeled "Don't Throw It Away".

3. Use the basket as motivation for a group discussion devoted to the need to recycle materials whenever possible as an aid to conservation of natural resources. Guide the discussion to draw on student experiences and observations related to waste, ugliness of discarded items along roadsides, etc.

4. Call attention to the fact that each of the packages is attractively wrapped with "used" materials and that the package contents would ordinarily be disposed of. Explain that each item has been selected because of its potential reuse.

5. Ask the students to take a package from the basket home (still wrapped) at the end of the day. Set aside three days for each student to devise at least five ways in which the item could be reused.

6. Convene the entire group on the appointed day and provide time for each student to present his or her item and the plans for reuse. Urge students to be as creative as possible and to present patterns, diagrams, sketches, and specific instructions whenever possible.

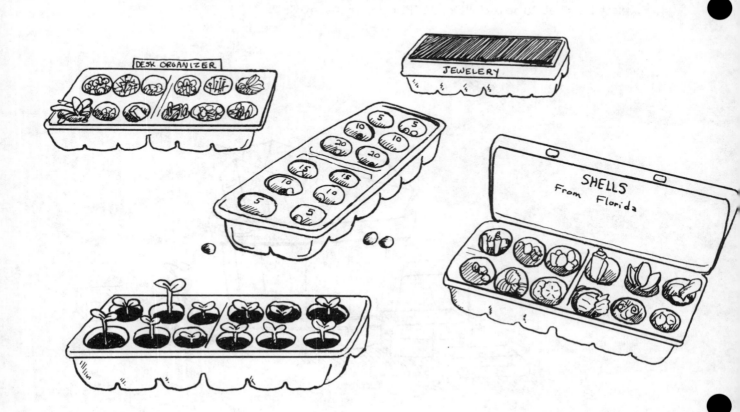

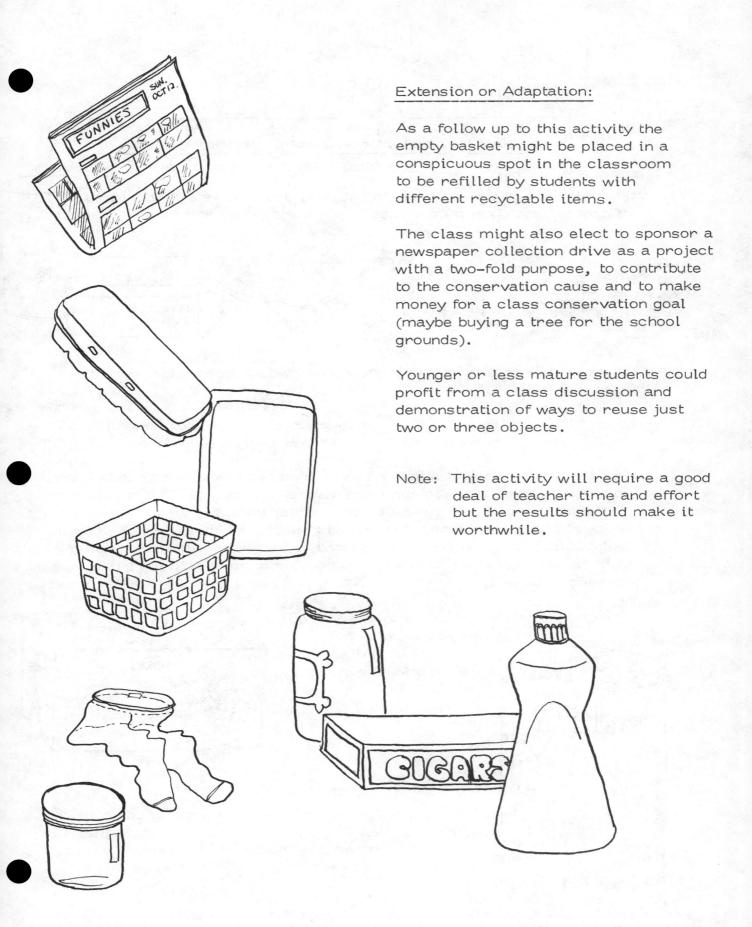

Extension or Adaptation:

As a follow up to this activity the empty basket might be placed in a conspicuous spot in the classroom to be refilled by students with different recyclable items.

The class might also elect to sponsor a newspaper collection drive as a project with a two-fold purpose, to contribute to the conservation cause and to make money for a class conservation goal (maybe buying a tree for the school grounds).

Younger or less mature students could profit from a class discussion and demonstration of ways to reuse just two or three objects.

Note: This activity will require a good deal of teacher time and effort but the results should make it worthwhile.

## EMOTION NOTIONS

Purpose:  After completing this activity the student should be able to relate to visual expression of a specific emotion.

1. Provide shoe boxes, oatmeal containers, and other sturdy boxes of appropriate size, a collection of old magazines, scissors, and paste.

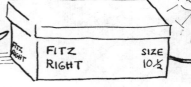

2. Direct students to form small groups and select an emotion from the following list:

| | | | |
|---|---|---|---|
| anger | fear | suspense | happiness |
| joy | surprise | sadness | tenderness |

3. Ask the group to select a box to use as the base of a diorama to be constructed in collage fashion from magazine clippings.  The discussion that takes place as various pictures, words, phrases, and other illustrations are presented for inclusion in the design will serve to help individuals within the group clarify and refine their own interpretation of the specific emotion as well as to provide insights into the subjective thinking of others.

The completed dioramas will make an attractive focal point for continuing discussion and emotional exploration.

Adaptation:

The format for the above activity could be applied to the study of countries and cities, famous people, historical or current events, state or national parks, or holidays.

FAMILY TREE TOPPER Work Sheet – Page 2

Name _____

1.  Find out and list the birth date and birth place of each person
    on your family tree.

    _____

    _____

    _____

    _____

2.  Use the dates to make a family time line representative of the
    persons shown on your family tree.

3.  How many years ago was the oldest person on your family tree
    born?  Where was he or she born? _____

4.  How many years older is the oldest living member of your family
    tree than the youngest living member?
    How well do they know each other? _____
    _____

5.  How many years older is the oldest living member of your family
    than you? _____  Write the most interesting fact
    that you know about this person. _____
    _____
    _____

6.  Select one person from your family tree who was born at least
    fifty years before you were to use as the subject of a biography.
    Ask questions of family members, do library research to learn
    what was happening in the world at the time of his or her birth and
    during his or her youth, and use reference books to locate
    information about the birthplace, types of transportation, local
    customs, and other interesting facts.  Write the biography and
    illustrate it with actual snapshots or portraits if available, or
    with original pen and ink sketches.

FRIENDSHIP SPECIAL

Purpose: After completing this activity the student should be able to demonstrate understanding of the value and responsibility of friendship.

1.  Provide chart paper and marker or chalk board and chalk along with a variety of art materials and scraps for students.

2.  Seat students in small circular groups of five or six. (Try to avoid placing "best friends" in the same circle.)

3.  Use the following procedure to introduce the list of Thought Questions:

    (1) Read the question slowly and carefully.

    (2) Ask students to think about the answer silently for a full minute.

    (3) When the teacher indicates thinking time is up, ask the students to share their answers honestly and quietly with their group by taking turns around the circle.

    (4) The teacher should call time when groups have had sufficient time to share.

4.  Ask students to return to normal seats.

5.  Ask recorders to share word lists aloud as the teacher writes them on the chart or board. Discuss each quality or attribute as it is given.

6.  Tell students that they will be given time (either immediately following this activity or at some later specified time) to create a THANK-YOU-FOR-BEING-MY-FRIEND gift. It can be any small thing--a card,

a homemade gift, a note indicating something special they will do for the friend, etc. just to say "thank you". What is chosen does not need to be shared with the class. Let it be a special, private gift to be enjoyed by the two friends. (Note: Be sure to tell students that the chosen friend does not need to be a classmate.)

THOUGHT QUESTIONS

1. Who are two of your very best friends? Name them.

2. Why do you like having each of them as a friend? What do they contribute to your life?

3. Why do you think each of them likes having you as a friend?

4. Is each friendship a fair exchange, or does one person have to give more or work harder than the other to be a part of it?

5. Choose one person in your group who is a good writer and speller to be your recorder. He or she will write down the answers to the next question. I am going to ask each person to think of at least three one-word answers to this question. Ready?

What does a person need to be like to be a good friend?
(Examples: kindness or kind, acceptance or accepting, honesty or honest)

After you have thought about your answers, the recorder will write down your words. If someone else has already given your answers, try to think of others or just give those that are new.

GUESS HOW I FEEL

Purpose:     After completing this activity the student should be able
             to express awareness of and sensitivity to human emotions.

1.   Lead a group discussion of different human emotions and their
     influence on individual and group behavior.  Guide the discussion
     to encourage individual student participation by asking students
     to contribute personal experiences and observations.  List
     emotions on the chalk board or a chart as they are presented
     for discussion.

fear                ANGER!              happiness
love                anxiety             frustration
hate                sadness               depression

2.   Provide large sheets of finger paint paper and finger paint in a <u>wide</u>
     variety of colors.

3.   Instruct the students to select one of the emotions listed on the board
     to portray in a finger painting.  Encourage them to mix colors and to
     use a variety of hand and finger movements to give as much "feeling"
     as possible to the paintings.

4.   Arrange the dry paintings attractively on a bulletin board.  Provide
     strips of paper to be used by students to guess at the feeling expressed
     in each painting.  Instruct students to pin their "guess" under each
     painting.

5.   Use the bulletin board display as the focal point of a follow-up
     discussion of emotions expressed.  Encourage each painter to
     discuss the intent of his or her painting and react to guesses related
     to it.

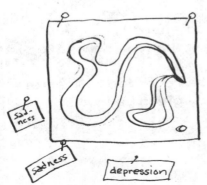 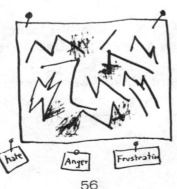 

# HAPPY BIRTHDAY TO ME

Purpose: After completing this activity the student should be able to identify significant items and concurrent historical events related to his own birth date.

1. Ask students to bring from home an empty box with a cover at least as large as a shoe box.

2. Explain that these boxes are special "birthday boxes". Each student is to use scraps to decorate the outside of his box to be representative of his personality and personal likes.

3. Have special information related to the birth date of the student placed inside each box:

   (1) Birth date

   (2) Astrological sign

   (3) Birthstone

   (4) Flower of the birth month

   (5) A record of historical events which coincide with this date, i.e., famous people born on this date, or anything else that happened on his date which the student would like to note

   (6) A favorite poem, story, or special game that might be played at a birthday party

   (7) A favorite recipe for a birthday dinner

   (8) A personal treasure (i.e., a shell, rock, picture, etc.)

4. Encourage each student to organize the above information in his own way, using both the inside cover of the box and the inside lining and space. A cut paper flower, a simulated birthstone, a "parchment" roll containing historical events, etc. will add special significance and interest to the collection.

5. Arrange a time for a special debut or presentation party after each student has completed his birthday box so that he may share its contents with the class if he wishes.

6. Provide a large birthday cake and a beverage and sing "Happy Birthday To All Of Us" at the close of this sharing time. Let students keep their boxes and encourage them to continue to use them as personal "treasure" boxes.

## HELPERS UNLIMITED

Purpose:  After completing this activity the student should be able to see himself as a valuable and interdependent member of the family, the immediate social environment, and the community.

1.  Discuss with students what things they as very young members of the family and community can do to improve or facilitate things for the family or community.

2.  Ask each student to identify one thing he or she could do to help another member of the family.  (A list of these may be made on a chart or chalk board if desired.)

3.  Ask each student to identify next one thing he or she could do for a friend or acquaintance outside the family unit.

4.  Ask students then to identify things that they could do to make changes or improvements in the community.

5.  Give students direction and guidance necessary in completing a personal contract in which each commits himself to at least one task contributing assistance or improvement in each of the above areas.  (See example on next page.)

6.  Have students report the results of their activities at a later date.

Note:  Excellent suggestions for activities and projects related to environmental change may be found in A Young Child Experiences by Kaplan et al (see Bibliography).

# HELPER'S CONTRACT

I, _____,

agree to fulfill the following commitments to my

family, friends, and community.


Family member I will help: _____

For this person, I will _____

_____

_____

_____


Another acquaintance I will help: _____

For this person, I will _____

_____

_____


One thing I will do for the improvement of my

community is _____

_____

_____

# A HOME IS MORE THAN A HOUSE

Purpose:
After completing this activity the student should be able to express awareness of differences in types of homes occupied by families.

1.  Provide magazines, paste, mural paper, and felt tip markers.

2.  Lead a group discussion of the many different types of homes occupied by families. (The discussion may be limited to the community or be as global in nature as the students' interests and experiences warrant.) List different types of homes on the chalk board as they are mentioned:

    apartment houses           high-rise condominiums
    mobile homes               converted barns
    duplexes                   town houses
    one-story houses           castles
    two-story houses           houseboats

3.  Ask each student to look through the magazines to find pictures of at least three different types of homes to be cut out and added to the class mural.

4.  Use felt tip markers to print labels for the various types of homes represented and to entitle the mural "A Home Is More Than A House" after the mural paper is completely filled.

5.  Display the mural in a conspicuous area of the classroom to be used to motivate discussion, creative writing, or role playing activities.

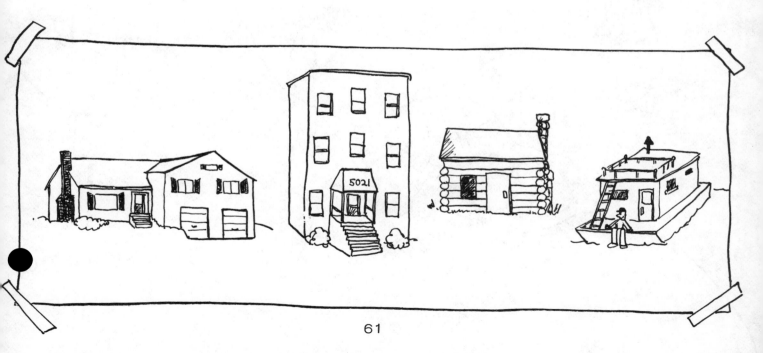

# I GET THE MESSAGE!

Purpose: After completing this activity the student should be able to identify many ways in which people communicate with one another.

1. Use the preceding pages to duplicate a communications picture for each student, or use these pages on a projector to create a mural-size representation.

2. Discuss with students the meaning of the word communication. Point out that there are hundreds of ways to get a message across to someone. (You might illustrate by using the message "come here": (1) motioning with hand, (2) holding up sign, (3) speaking the words, etc.

3. Explain that you have prepared a special picture that shows communication in everyday life. Ask them to look carefully at it and point out each place they see some means of communication.

4. Let students label these parts individually or work in pairs at a large mural. Younger students may merely use X's and explain their choices orally. Older students may use labels such as is done on the marked teacher-key copy of the communications picture.

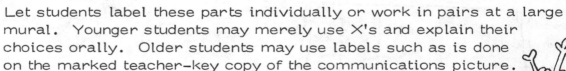

## LOOK AT ME

Purpose: | After completing this activity the student should be able to develop and express awareness of self and others.

1. Provide large sheets of brown butcher paper, crayons, felt tip markers, scissors, and masking tape.

2. Ask the student to lie flat on the paper while the teacher or another student traces around the body.

3. Direct the student to cut carefully around the completed outline to form a life-size paper doll. Encourage the student to look in the mirror and ask friends to help make judgments about the color of his or her eyes and hair, and how the paper doll can be given real personality.

4. Provide time for the paper doll to be attractively completed, and assist the student in displaying the self-replica in a designated spot.

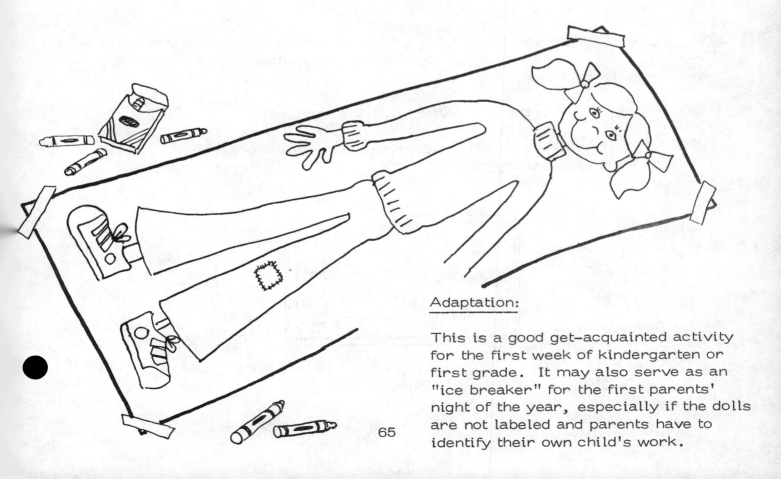

Adaptation:

This is a good get-acquainted activity for the first week of kindergarten or first grade. It may also serve as an "ice breaker" for the first parents' night of the year, especially if the dolls are not labeled and parents have to identify their own child's work.

65

Purpose:    After completing this activity the student should be able
            to create on paper a symbolic representation of a real
            place.

1.    Provide two shoe boxes identical in size, two identical sets of doll
      furniture, several 5 x 7" cards for instructions and answers, a
      red marker, and a blue marker.  In addition, prepare one card
      or a piece of heavy paper cut to the same size as the top surface of
      the shoe box for each student.

2.    Use one set of the doll furniture to create a room arrangement on the
      inside of one shoe box lid.

3.    Use glue to fix these pieces
      in place, leaving at least 1/4"
      around the outside edge, so
      that the lid may be replaced
      on the box.

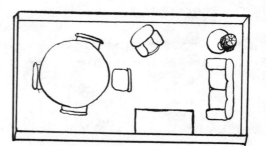

4.    Cover the lid with the bottom
      of the box.  (Of course, the
      box will now be upside down.)
      Mark the box with a large red
      circle.

5.    Place the second set of doll furniture in the other shoe box.  Mark the
      box with a blue circle.  Add a 5 x 7" card bearing the following
      instructions:

      (1)    Open the box marked with the red circle.

      (2)    Look carefully at the way the furniture is arranged in this
             imaginary room.

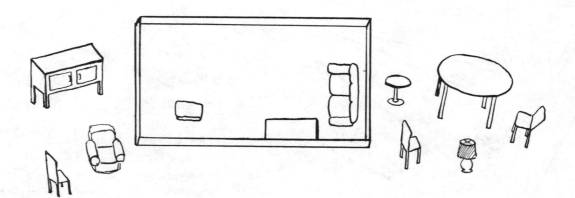

66

(3)  Use the furniture and the lid of the box marked with the blue circle to make a room which looks exactly like the room in the red box.

(4)  Ask someone to check your work to be sure it is exactly right.

(5)  Use one of the large cards in this box to make a map of the room you have just set up.  (You might do this by laying your card parallel to the box lid and drawing a circle, square, or rectangle, etc. to represent each piece of furniture.  Be sure you draw it just about the same size and put it in exactly the right place.)

(6)  Compare your drawing to the one in the answer envelope.

6.  Add an "answer" card in an envelope so that students may use it to check their work.

7.  Place the boxes in a learning center or area where all students may spread them out for easy use.

8.  Introduce the activity to the group by showing the boxes, explaining directions, and actually doing at least part of the activity.  Students should be able to complete the activity on their own.

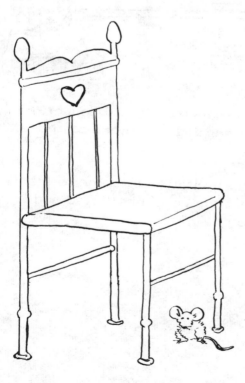

Adaptation:

The above activity may be done with symbols and oral instruction only for use with very young children.

# MY KIND OF TOWN

Purpose:   After completing this activity the student should be able
to identify current needs of the community in which he
lives.

1.   Use the streets, buildings, and other features of the Box Town
model as the basis for a class discussion of features unique to
the local community.

2.   Divide the chalk board into two sections.  Label one section
"Good for our Town" and one section "Our Town Needs".  Lead
the discussion to include attention to strengths and weaknesses
and encourage students to verbalize both positive and negative
observations.  List student responses in the appropriate space.

Good For Our Town

Civic Auditorium
Good Roads
Modern Shopping Center

Our Town Needs

Bike Trails
Better Drainage
New Library
More Traffic Signs

3.   Ask each student to write a letter to the mayor or a city councilman
stating interest in community improvement and citing one or more
of the concerns listed.

4.   Mail the letters to the addressee with an invitation to come to the
classroom to talk with the students about the concerns listed and
the problems involved in correcting them.

# NATURAL RESOURCE #1

**Purpose:** After completing this activity the student should be able to perceive himself as a valuable composite of resources on which he can build and rely.

1. Prepare a copy of the following page for each student.

2. Ask each student to consider himself or herself as a resource for economic power. What can he do? What marketable skills does he have? What can he produce that someone else might use?

3. Discuss as a class; then ask students to use scrap paper to list things they can do; i.e., cook, sew, scrub, paint, rake leaves, deliver papers, run errands, do housework, read, clip papers or magazines, write, draw, dance, sing, talk, make calls, make signs.

   Spark their thinking by asking them to consider (1) what they could do for older people, (2) what they could do around home to help their parents, (3) what they could do for younger children or how they might help kids their own age (tutoring, reading to, taking notes for, etc.), and (4) what items they could make for sale and who would buy them.

4. Ask students to consider what tools they have at their disposal to accomplish some of the things they can do. They should list these on scrap paper (things such as lawnmower, hammer, cooking utensils, needle and thread, telephone, bicycle, etc.).

5. Ask them to use the following student page to list their skills and tools. When they have finished they may paste the page on a piece of heavy construction paper or tagboard, cut it out, and decorate the reverse side with crayon or cut paper to look like themselves.

6. Hang these by string from the ceiling over each student's desk. Reinforce for several days the idea that "we have a roomful of marvelous human resource and potential". Use this activity to inspire confidence, pride, and self—worth in each individual.

69

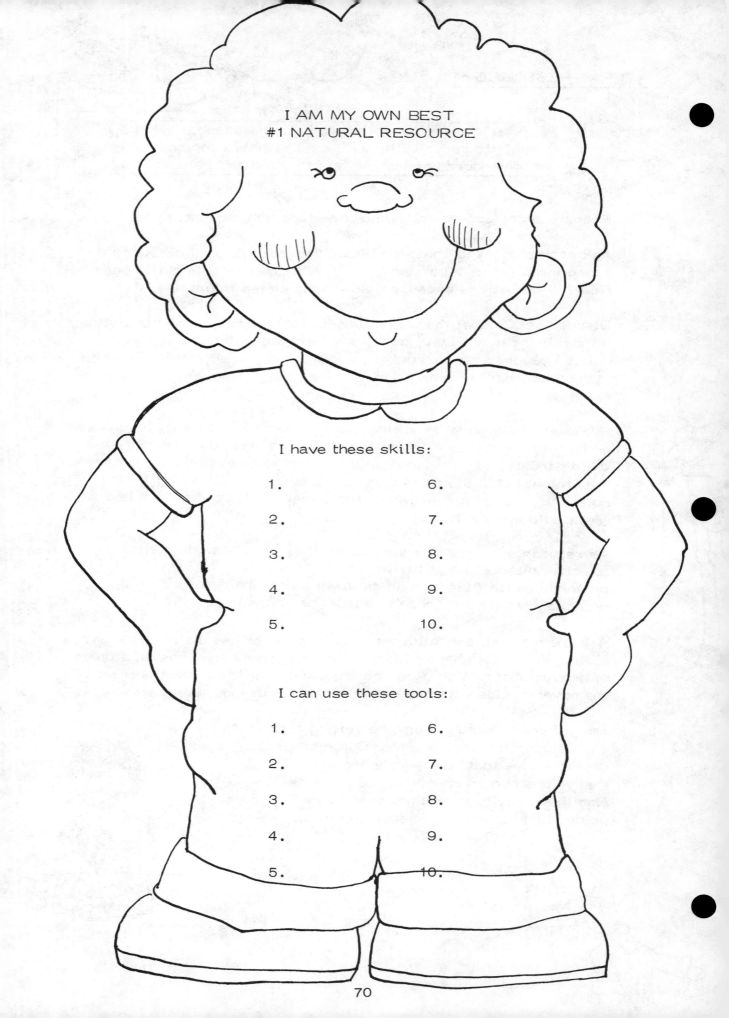

I AM MY OWN BEST
#1 NATURAL RESOURCE

I have these skills:

1.                    6.

2.                    7.

3.                    8.

4.                    9.

5.                    10.

I can use these tools:

1.                    6.

2.                    7.

3.                    8.

4.                    9.

5.                    10.

70

# NUMBER PLEASE

Purpose: 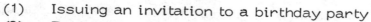 After completing this activity the student should be able to use the telephone correctly.

1.    Provide two toy telephones, drawing paper, and crayons.

2.    Print subjects for telephone conversations on strips of tagboard, such as:

      (1)    Issuing an invitation to a birthday party
      (2)    Reporting a fire
      (3)    Taking a message for another member of the family
      (4)    Asking a classmate for a homework assignment
      (5)    Placing a grocery order
      (6)    Calling for the doctor in an emergency
      (7)    Calling someone on business during office hours
      (8)    Reporting a power failure to the electric company
      (9)    Notifying the school of your illness
    (10)    Declining a picnic invitation

3.    Assemble a small group of students in a circle in a quiet corner of the classroom.

4.    Turn the sentence strips face down on a table in the center of the circle and place the phones on the table.

5.    Ask one student to take a sentence strip and select a classmate to role play the situation in a phone conversation.  The other students will enjoy and profit from critiqueing the conversation after it is completed.

Adaptation and Extension:

This activity could be extended to include a bulletin board display featuring good telephone manners or an experience chart developed by the group to give some "dos and don'ts" for telephone conversations.

PEOPLE IN THE KNOW

Purpose: After completing this activity the student should be able to use interview techniques and organize data to contribute to a human resources file.

1. Review the scope of the year's projected social studies curriculum with the class early in the school year. Involve students as much as possible in planning the sequence and procedure to be followed. List major topics of study and highlights of the program on the chalk board as they are discussed. Encourage individual students to contribute suggestions for unique approaches to studying various areas and to propose special projects and group activities.

2. Ask one student to serve as recorder to be responsible for recording all suggestions and later copying the compiled list for future reference. The list may be duplicated and distributed to students as a "work sheet".

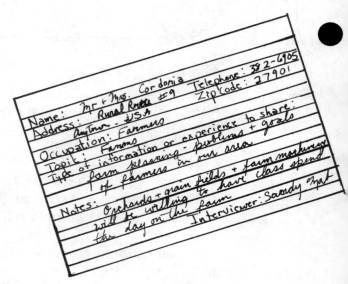

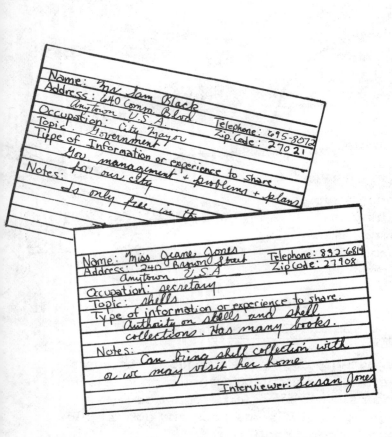

3. As the topics of study and the projects are identified, guide the discussion to focus on materials available and on people in the community who may be able to serve as special resource people. Encourage each student to contribute to this list by adding names of relatives, neighbors, or friends that may not be known to other students.

4.  Provide a 4 x 6" card box and a supply of cards. Explain to the students that the box is to be used as a resource file to contain specific information relevant to people in the community who will be willing to contribute some time and talent to the class during the coming school year.

5.  Develop the format to be used in gathering and compiling information for the file as a part of the group discussion.

Name:
Address:                                  Telephone:
                                          Zip Code:
Occupation:
Topic
Type of information or experience to share.

Notes: (use back of card if necessary)

                    Interviewer:

6.  Ask each student to be responsible for interviewing one person and completing the card for the resource file. (Name people to be interviewed in order to avoid duplication.)

7.  Maintain and update the file during the school year. As different topics of study are undertaken, the student whose name is on the appropriate card as interviewer may be called on to make the contact, issue the invitation, introduce the person to the class, and assume responsibility for the follow-up discussion and thank-you notes.

## POP-UP HELPERS

Purpose: After completing this activity the student should be able to identify community helpers and describe their functions in the community setting.

1. Use story books and pictures to introduce names and jobs of community helpers.

2. Discuss how each does his job and emphasize the importance of that person to the community. (Invite as many of these people as possible to visit the classroom.)

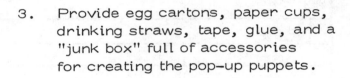

3. Provide egg cartons, paper cups, drinking straws, tape, glue, and a "junk box" full of accessories for creating the pop-up puppets.

4. Ask each student to choose at least one community helper and create a pop-up puppet likeness of that person in the following manner:

(1) Use one section or cup of an egg carton to create a face. (Features may be drawn directly on the cup or they may be glued on.)

(2) Add hair, eyes, ears, hats, collars, etc. by using odd pieces of material, yarn, buttons, etc. from the "junk box".

(3) Glue or tape the finished face to the top of a drinking straw.

(4) Make a hole in the center bottom of a drinking cup and insert the bottom of the straw.

(5) Push the straw up and down and your puppet-helper will appear and disappear.

5.  Encourage students to work in small groups to create short puppet shows involving their puppets in dramatic situations that demonstrate their job opportunities. (A cardboard box may be used to create a puppet stage or theatre.)

## TASTE AND TELL

Purpose: After completing this activity the student should be able to demonstrate knowledge and appreciation of a variety of foods as reflective of family culture and social mores.

1. Provide reference books, writing paper, pencils, art supplies, paper plates, cups, and plastic picnic forks and spoons.

2. Arrange time for a group discussion of differing tastes in foods and family mealtime habits. Encourage students to name foods that are special in their own families, and to discuss the background of the food and tell why it has become a family favorite.

3.  Set aside a day for "Taste and Tell" and ask each student to bring a favorite family recipe and food prepared according to the recipe to share with the class. Teachers will want to exercise caution to make sure students who may not be able to bring food from home have opportunity to share in the activity in a positive sense. Make plans for a festive tasting session, and encourage free dialogue to foster new concepts related to the uniqueness of the taste, origin, and preparation of the food.

4.  Type or print the recipes attractively to reproduce copies for each student to include in a special recipe book to take home. (See the steps for making a book on the following page.)

Adaptation and Extension:

This would be a good activity for a Thanksgiving follow-up to the story of the Pilgrims and Indians sharing food as a means of becoming better acquainted. It would also serve as a culminating activity for a study of foods, production, of varying family life styles, or of various cultural holidays. The recipe book would make a nice Mother's Day or Christmas gift.

77

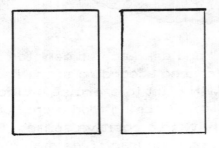

1. Using two pieces of cardboard for the cover, place them on a table side by side, leaving about an inch of space between them.

2. Now pull off a long piece of masking tape and tear it into 10 or 12 small pieces about 4" long, and stick the edges of them onto the side of the desk or table, just for your convenience in placing them on the book.

3. Place the strips of tape on the book, like this:

4. Turn the whole thing over--the two pieces of cardboard, stripped with tape--and repeat the tape procedure

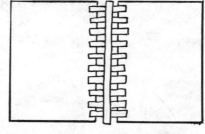

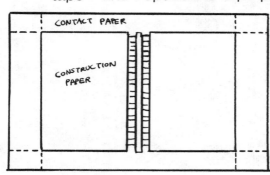

on the reverse side. Now put a piece of masking tape down the center of the cross pieces, on each side.

5. Cut a piece of contact paper large enough so that it will extend past each edge of the cover about 2" and carefully place the cardboard cover in the center.

6. Place a piece of construction paper on each piece of cardboard. It will adhere to the cardboard when the contact paper is folded onto it.

7. Now it will look like the drawing below. Pretend you have used striped contact paper.

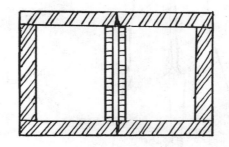

# TOOL BOXERS

Purpose: After completing this activity the student should be able to name and categorize tools associated with specified occupations.

1. Reproduce copies of the Tool Boxers Work Sheet on the following page.

2. Provide resource books (see Bibliography), pencils, crayons, and Tool Boxers Work Sheets.

3. Instruct the student to use resource books as needed to complete the work sheet.

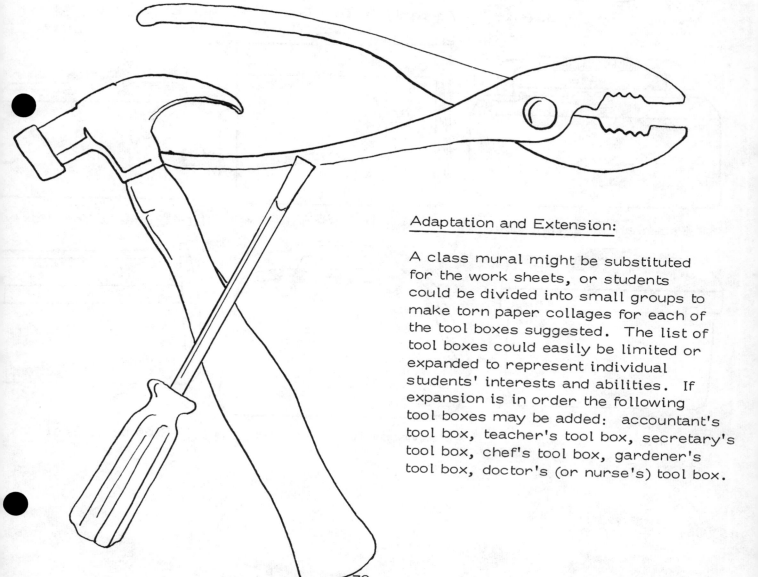

## Adaptation and Extension:

A class mural might be substituted for the work sheets, or students could be divided into small groups to make torn paper collages for each of the tool boxes suggested. The list of tool boxes could easily be limited or expanded to represent individual students' interests and abilities. If expansion is in order the following tool boxes may be added: accountant's tool box, teacher's tool box, secretary's tool box, chef's tool box, gardener's tool box, doctor's (or nurse's) tool box.

# TOOL BOXERS WORK SHEET

Draw pictures or print the names of at least five tools that you would expect to find in each of these tool boxes.

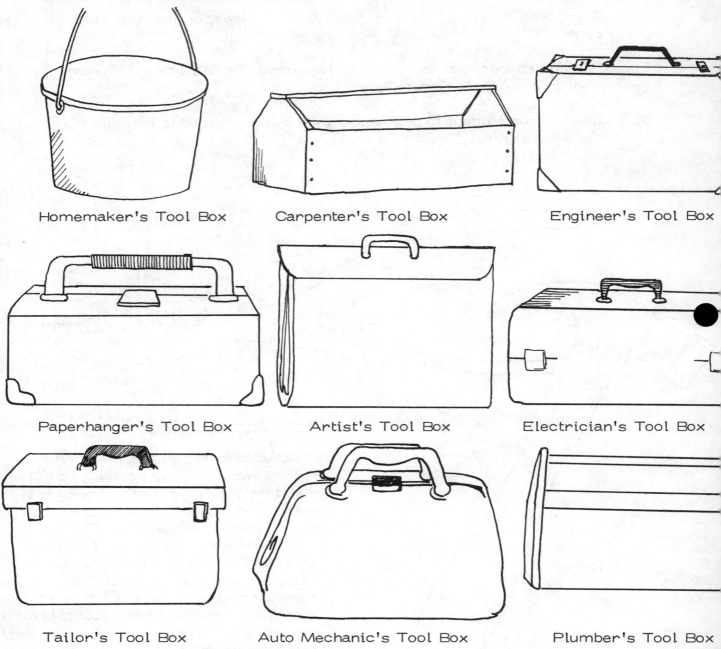

Homemaker's Tool Box     Carpenter's Tool Box     Engineer's Tool Box

Paperhanger's Tool Box     Artist's Tool Box     Electrician's Tool Box

Tailor's Tool Box     Auto Mechanic's Tool Box     Plumber's Tool Box

## UNBURIED TREASURES

Purpose: | After completing this activity the student should be able to express awareness and appreciation of unique features of the community.

1.  Lead a class discussion dealing with the community as it is perceived by members of the group. Ask questions to motivate comments concerning buildings, scenic spots, areas of special pride, social situations, and resources unique to the community.

2.  Distribute copies of the work sheet on the following page and ask the students to use it as a guide for a treasure hunt to locate features of the community that have been overlooked or taken for granted. Instruct them to write a brief "descriptive clue" for each feature to better identify it for their classmates.

3.  Set aside three or four days for completion of the work sheets. Caution the students to take time to think carefully about each item and to write their clues interestingly to provoke sensitivity to the people and places cited.

4.  Arrange a time for sharing the perceptions in a group setting upon completion of the work sheets.

5.  Culminate the activity by asking each student to creatively portray one special feature of the community for inclusion in a class "community pride showcase" to be shared with other classes. This collection could include poetry, paintings, songs, collages, historical or sociological accounts, biographies, descriptive narratives, sculptures, dioramas, drawings, etc.

UNBURIED TREASURES – Work Sheet

1.  The most beautiful spot in our community for a picnic is

    _____

    _____

2.  I found five different kinds of trees growing.  The names of the
    five trees are:

    _____  _____  _____  _____  _____

3.  A very unusual building is located _____

    _____

    _____

4.  One important natural resource of our community is _____

    _____

    _____

5.  If I had a visitor from another country I would especially like to show

    _____

    _____

6.  A person our community can be proud of is _____

    _____

    _____

7.  On an early morning walk in the community you could enjoy

    _____

    _____

8.  A street showing the home owner's pride is _____

9. I think the most colorful character in our community is

_____

_____

10. A city official that I admire is _____

_____

11. If I could give a medal to the person I think has made the greatest contribution to our community I'd give it to

_____

12. One very important thing that happened in our community during the past year was

_____

_____

13. The tallest building in our community is _____

_____

14. Our community fights pollution by _____

_____

_____

15. The very nicest thing that I can say about my community is

_____

_____

_____

_____

# VARIATIONS ON VALUES

Purpose:      After completing this activity the student should be able to assess his own personal values and make a conscious effort to order or reorder his priorities.

1.     Cut from magazines at least ten large, colorful pictures that show people engaged in activities that demonstrate something about their personal values (or show what things might be of importance to them).

2.     Paste these pictures (one to a page) in a large scrapbook. Add a title page that says "Variations On Values" or some similar title.

3.     Instruct students to use the scrapbook individually, to look at each picture carefully, and to decide what kinds of qualities are paramount or most important to the people in the pictures. Then they should write words or sentences that represent these ideas on the back of the page bearing that picture. (All students will thus be adding their assessments to the same page.) Written instructions may appear on an introductory page or at the top of each page--or may be given orally.

4.  Add to the scrapbook a page for each student who will use this book. Put the student's name at the top of the page in bold letters.

5.  Ask each student to find the page bearing his name after he has finished viewing and making comments on the picture pages. On that page ask him to draw or paste cut-out pictures that represent things and qualities that are of special value to him.

6.  Have the students review the scrapbook at a later date and add comments to the reverse side of these pages just as they did to the beginning picture pages.

Conduct a class discussion related to personal values before the scrapbook is discarded or added to the classroom library for further review and thought. Let each student name at least one thing of paramount importance to him.

Write these on the chalk board or on a large chart entitled "What's Important?"

## WHOSE BAG?

Purpose:  After completing this activity the student should be able to demonstrate awareness of unique personality differences within a group.

1.  Distribute plain brown paper bags to the students the day before this activity is to take place.

2.  Ask each student to take a bag home and fill it with articles to tell the story of his identity.  Instruct them to select five articles that they feel are reflective of their own personalities.

3.  Have the students place the filled and unmarked bags on the teacher's desk as they arrive the next morning.

4.  The bags are then randomly distributed and at a signal from the teacher the bags are opened.

5.  Have each student take a turn to display the items in his bag and to try to identify the person who prepared the bag.

The degree of accuracy in identification of the owners of the various bags will be amazing, and will serve to reinforce self concepts within the group.

## WRITE ALL ABOUT IT!

Purpose: After completing this activity the student should be able to assist in the conception, production, and distribution of a newspaper.

1.  Assemble a large collection of newspapers (including national, state, local, school, and specialized).

2.  Ask the students to examine the newspapers carefully, giving attention to regular and special editions; commonalities and differences, make-up and layout, and other features.

3.  Guide the group in planning, organizing, and volunteering for individual work tasks leading to the development of a school newspaper. As an outgrowth of the group discussion, list responsibilities on the chalk board:

    | | |
    |---|---|
    | editor | copy editors |
    | associate editor | layout |
    | feature editors | advertising |
    | reporters | production |
    | circulation | |

4.  Stress the importance of accuracy in reporting, word usage, sentence structure, writing to convey a message or meaning, and meeting deadlines. When each student has accepted a specific assignment, establish a deadline for task completion and make arrangements for assembling, typing, and reproducing the newspaper.

5.  Establish a nominal price for the newspaper and arrange to sell copies to students in other classes.

Extension and Adaptation:

Teachers and students may wish to select one or more of the following suggestions as motivation or follow-up activities:

(1)     Write articles about the school to be submitted to the local newspaper.

(2)     Prepare a quiz (multiple choice, true/false, and short narrative questions) and ask each student to use the daily newspaper to find answers.

(3)     Write letters to the editor of either the school or local newspaper.

(4)     Make a list of five significant topics of concern to the class covered in one of the newspapers used in this activity. Compare student opinions on "significant topics" and allow time for an in-depth discussion of differences of opinions.

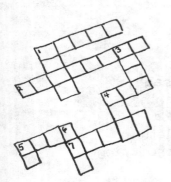

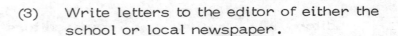

(5)     Ask each student to devise a crossword puzzle for the class newspaper based on a social studies topic of interest to the group.

(6)     Select one article from the newspaper and design a cartoon strip with dialogue to present the article more clearly.

(7)     Elect a student committee to evaluate the accuracy, graphics, interest, appeal, and cost of each newspaper in the collection.

(8)     Plan and prepare a special edition news sheet devoted to the school's art, music, library, or physical education program.

(9)     Write reviews of books of current social studies interest to be included in the classroom newspaper.

(10)    Plan a newspaper for the year 2001.

THIS IS STATION WXZY BROADCASTING LIVE FROM....

(11) Write radio and/or television newscasts based on the daily news as reported in the newspapers.

(12) Select one article from the local newspaper and conduct a public opinion poll in the school. Report the findings of the poll in the class newspaper.

(13) Select want ads that tell something about life today, and discuss the circumstances that led to placing the ad and the reasons why readers will or will not respond to it.

# HILL SCHOOL NEWS

✳ JANUARY 12 ······························· COPY NUMBER 9  ✳

BASKETBALL CHEERLEADERS CHOSEN!

MR. SMITH RETIRES▭

SAFETY PATROLS CONGRATULATED ON GREAT WORK

ROOM #105 WINS GYM DAY TROPHY!!

SPORT SCENE

RAIDERS WIN 12-3

# notes .....

notes . . . .

# AMERICANS ON THE MOVE

Purpose: After completing this activity the student should be able to demonstrate understanding and awareness of the common mobility of Americans.

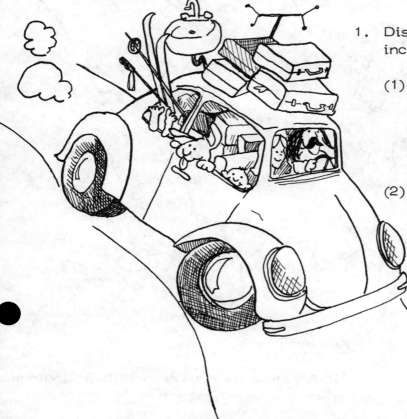

1. Discuss with the students the high incidence of mobility in the United States.

   (1) Ask how many students have lived in some other city or state. Locate those places on the large map and estimate mileage from that place to your city or town.

   (2) Ask how many students' parents once lived in another place. Locate and estimate mileage from those places.

2. Provide a copy of the following map to each student. Ask him to identify places where he, a member of his family, or a person of his acquaintance has lived.

3. The student should mark each of these places with an "X" or asterisk and write in the name of the town, city, and state.

4. Then, using a different color pencil or crayon for each person or family, draw an arrow from the previous residence to the present place of residence.

5. Ask students to try to identify at least six to ten such "moves" on their maps. (Parents may be helpful resources in providing information and identifying cities, etc.)

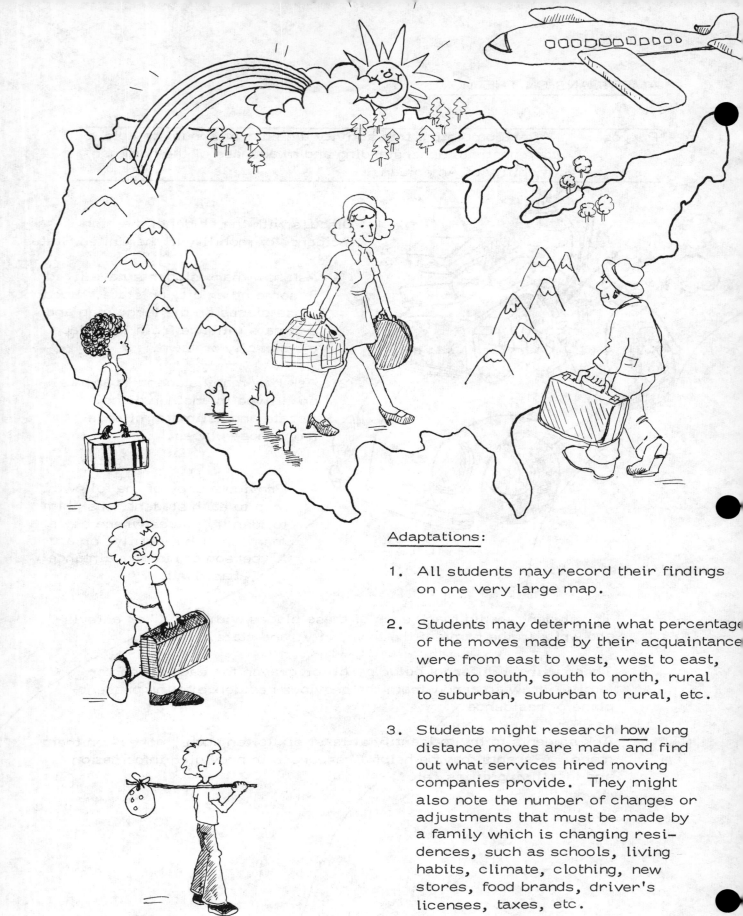

Adaptations:

1.  All students may record their findings on one very large map.

2.  Students may determine what percentage of the moves made by their acquaintances were from east to west, west to east, north to south, south to north, rural to suburban, suburban to rural, etc.

3.  Students might research how long distance moves are made and find out what services hired moving companies provide. They might also note the number of changes or adjustments that must be made by a family which is changing residences, such as schools, living habits, climate, clothing, new stores, food brands, driver's licenses, taxes, etc.

94

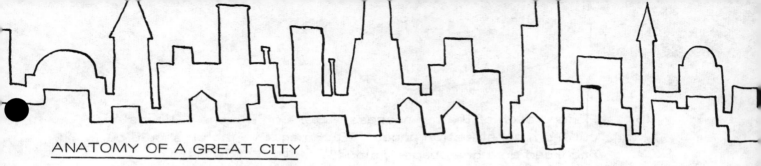

## ANATOMY OF A GREAT CITY

Purpose: After completing this activity the student should be able to demonstrate increased knowledge, awareness, and appreciation for the great cities of the United States and for his own city.

1. Secure copies of several of the well-known songs and poems written about American cities:

> Carl Sandburg's "Chicago"
> "Meet Me in St. Louis"
> "New York, New York (What a Wonderful Town)"
> "I Left My Heart in San Francisco"

2. Read and sing these to the students or let students or groups of students prepare to present several of these to the class.

3. Discuss the characteristics common to all of these poetic pieces. (Each describes the city in some way. It tells something of its industry, its geography, its people, its climate, what there is to do there, etc.)

4. Ask each student then to choose one of the following cities (or one not listed but approved by the teacher):

| | |
|---|---|
| New York | San Francisco |
| Atlanta | St. Louis |
| Dallas | Boston |
| Salt Lake City | New Orleans |
| Phoenix | Chicago |

5. Provide resource materials and special library time for students to read about the city they have chosen.

As they read each should try to identify at least ten things about the chosen city that have contributed to its success or "made it great". (They might also identify at least one negative or "not-so-great" item about the city.)

6. Record each of the ten success factors on a large yellow star cut from construction paper. Each negative factor should be recorded on a grey paper "cloud".

7. Provide a wire coat hanger for each student. The body of the hanger should be artistically decorated and labeled by the student to identify the chosen city. Then the stars and clouds should be hung from the bottom of the hanger on       varied lengths of string, wire, or thread.

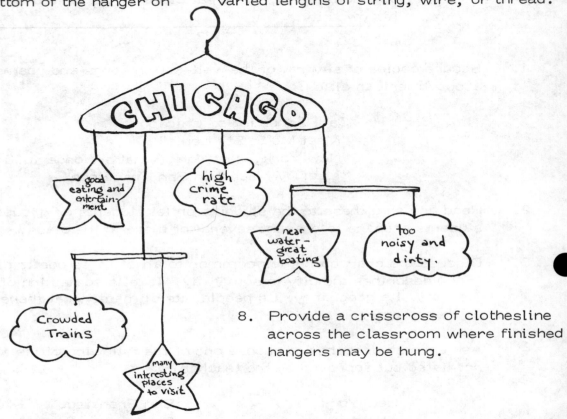

8. Provide a crisscross of clothesline across the classroom where finished hangers may be hung.

9. Ask each student to share his findings at a specially appointed time and justify at least three of his item choices.

10. Ask students to work together as a group or as individuals to write a song or poem about their own cities after information about these cities has been shared. These may be shared in a performance at a later time.

## AND ONE TO GROW ON

Purpose:  After completing this activity the student should be able to demonstrate understanding and appreciation of different phases of American history as reflected by centennial year customs and mores.

1.  Initiate a class discussion of the signing of the Declaration of Independence in 1776.  Encourage students to contribute ideas about the people and events associated with the first Independence Day celebration, and list them on the chalk board.

* Parades
* Feasting
* Candles/Lanterns
* Patriotic speeches
  glowing

2.  Develop this by writing 1776 above the festive events listed on the chalk board, and make a similar column for 1876, 1976, and 2076.  Explain to the students that centennial years have traditionally provided a good time for Americans to demonstrate appreciation for the rights and privileges of people of a free nation.

3.  Instruct the class to divide into four groups to plan four birthday parties to celebrate the nation's independence.  Set aside the last hour of the school day on four consecutive Fridays for the parties.

4.  Provide resource books (see Bibliography) and ask the students to investigate carefully the period their particular party is to represent. (The teacher will need to serve as consultant to each group as plans are being made.)  Ask each group to make its party as authentic and true to life as possible.  Planning party hats, food, favors, speeches, parades, games, songs, decorations, or other appropriately creative party activities will help both party planners and guests "feel" the spirit of the times.

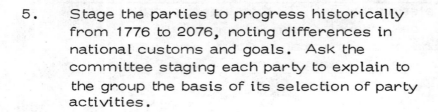

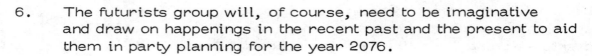

5.  Stage the parties to progress historically
    from 1776 to 2076, noting differences in
    national customs and goals.  Ask the
    committee staging each party to explain to
    the group the basis of its selection of party
    activities.

6.  The futurists group will, of course, need to be imaginative
    and draw on happenings in the recent past and the present to aid
    them in party planning for the year 2076.

7.  Compare notes on the four parties and the four periods of time
    they represent as a culminating activity.  Cite the influence of
    periods of industrial growth, wars, depressions, rapid educa-
    tional gains, transportation and communication, affluence,
    depletion of natural resources, and other factors on the way
    people have celebrated Independence Day in the past and may
    celebrate it in 2076.

### Extension and Adaptation:

As a fun extension of this activity, a
round hat box could be covered with
ivory soap flake paste (whip ivory soap
flakes with just a little water to form a
soft paste) to make a birthday cake to
which each group could add one red or
blue candle at the time of its party.

Designing costumes (on paper only),
writing invitations, thank you notes
and shopping lists, and making murals
could provide additional excitement.
Students might also enjoy selecting the
period in which they would most like to
live and write a story, poem, or play
to express their feelings about this time.

A simplified version of this activity might
culminate in only one party with each
group making one contribution, such as
1776 party hats, 1876 refreshments, 1976
parade with music and patroitic speeches,
and 2076 games and prizes.

# BALL O' YARNS

Purpose:  After completing this activity the student should be able to demonstrate increased appreciation for the freedom and openness of the American spirit and the delight its people find in humor and enjoyment.

1. Secure a copy of Carl Sandburg's poem, The People, Yes, specifically the passage from this poem pertaining to yarns told and retold in the folklore and fanciful literature of our country (see Bibliography).

2. Read aloud with entertaining exaggeration this portion of the poem for pure fun and enjoyment. Ask students to imagine the skyscraper with hinges, the old man whose whiskers arrived a day ahead of him, the snake who swallowed itself, Paul Bunyan's blue ox Babe, and Pecos Bill straddling a cyclone.

3. Reread the selection and ask them to try to remember one or two things especially amusing to them.

4. Provide time and materials for students to do one of the following related projects after these have been discussed and enjoyed:

   (1) Draw a panorama representing several of Sandburg's exaggerated yarns.

   (2) Write some imaginative exaggerated yarns of your own.

   (3) Create a shoe-box diorama representing a famous American folk-saying or tale.

   (4) Plan and present a short creative drama representing a piece of American folklore.

CLASSIFIED INFORMATION

Purpose: After completing this activity the student should be able to demonstrate knowledge and understanding of historic, geographic, economic, and sociological factors of importance to the United States.

1. Use the opaque or overhead projector to reproduce the map of the United States (see Appendix) on an old shower curtain or plastic tablecloth.

2. Place the map on the floor in a convenient spot. Provide red, white, and blue bean bags; red, white, and blue buttons to be used for tokens; and a placard with the following instructions:

---

## RULES

1) Two or more players may play this game.

2) Taking turns the players throw the bean bag onto the mat.

3) If the player can give one historical fact, one geographical fact, one economic fact, and one sociological fact about the state that the bean bag lands on, he or she may take 5 tokens. If the player is able to give facts in some of the required areas but not in all four, one token is earned for each area. (The extra token for giving all facts in all four areas is a "bonus".)

4) The game continues until one player earns thirty-five tokens to win the game.

---

Note: The object of this game is to encourage students to acquire and process facts about the states to be used when playing the game in their free time.

Adaptation:

Game directions for less mature students might require players to give only one fact without identifying the ar[...]

# CONSERVATION CONSULTANTS, INC.

Purpose: After completing this activity the student should be able to express creative ideas related to the responsibility of individual citizens to use natural resources wisely.

1. Provide reference books and pictures related to pollution and conservation of natural resources. Lead a group discussion on the importance of developing good conservation habits and on the consequences to all people if this is not done. Guide the discussion to focus on the individual citizen's responsibility and sphere of influence related to the immediate environment.

2. Ask students to name areas of ecological concern. List topics on the chalk board as they are suggested. Topics could include:

Saving Our Waterways from Pollution
Noise Pollution
Smoke and Smut: Public Enemies
Endangered Species: Animals
Endangered Species: Plants
How Clean Is Your Neighborhood?
America's National Parks: Whose Responsibility?
How Do We Reform Litterbugs?
Putting An End to Dirty Streets
Freeing America's Highways of Ugly Signs
How About Junk Cars?
No Smoking, Please!
Let's Start A Recycling Cycle
Overpopulation – Real or Imaginary

3. Aid the students in making plans to positively promote conservation in their own neighborhoods by forming a consulting firm dedicated to this cause. Discuss the role of a consultant, asking one student to look up the word in the dictionary and write it on the chalk board. Webster gives this definition:

Consultant – one who consults; one who offers business, professional, or expert advice for a fee

101

4.   Ask each student (or two students working together as a consulting team) to select one of the topics listed on the chalk board (or another topic approved by the group) to research and prepare for presentation from the "expert's" point of view and understanding. Emphasize the importance of consulting integrity as the basis for in-depth study and careful preparation of all ideas and materials for dissemination. Encourage organization of ideas and materials, development of brochures, questionnaires, and/or other audio and visual aids.

5.   Stage an election of officers and directors for the consulting firm. (Remind the students that these people will be responsible for coordinating and giving meaning and direction to the efforts of the total group.) Devote as much time as needed to group development of roles and role descriptions.

6.   After the election ask the elected officials to assume responsibility for the following tasks:

   (1)   Making a chart for public display carrying the names of offices and officers of Conservation Consultants, Inc. The chart should also contain the carefully stated purpose of the group.

   (2)   Reproducing and distributing badges and certificates to all members of the consulting group. Patterns for both will be found on the following page. The badge should be made from gold or silver gift wrap or yellow construction paper, lettered with a fine point felt tip pen, laminated or covered with clear contact paper and fastened to a safety pin with masking tape. The certificate may be reproduced and lettered for each consultant. (If the students elect to develop their own badges and certificates, congratulate them on their originality and provide materials and encouragement as needed).

   (3)   Preparing a complete listing of all consultants and their areas of expertise, i.e.:

           Shana MacKenzie:  Preserving America's Wildflowers
           Jennifer Farnette:  Feathering Nests for our Feathered
                                         Friends
           Julie Murphy:  Keeping Our Blue Skies Blue

(4)    Distributing copies of topics, consultants, and volunteer consulting services to other classes, Scout troops, the P.T.A., civic, and other appropriate groups.

(5)    Planning consulting activities, including time scheduling, arrangements, and follow-up.

THIS IS TO CERTIFY THAT

_____

as a member of Conservation Consultants, Inc.

is qualified in all respects to serve as a

consultant in good standing on _____

_____

_____

_____

_____

_____

_____

_____

104

## DAFFY DEFINITIONS

Purpose:
After completing this activity the student should be able to demonstrate a renewed appreciation for the sound and feel of language and enjoy relating it to the vocabulary of the social sciences.

1. Provide a copy of the following page for each student.

2. Read and say aloud with the class the nonsense words in Column I. Let them enjoy rolling them on their tongues--seeing how quickly they can re-read aloud to themselves the entire list.

3. Then read with them the words in Column II. Ask students to experiment with the two lists of words by trying to match each adjective in Column I with one of the nouns in Column II. They should try to match pairs that seem to "fit", "make sense", or "sound good" together.

4. When they have done this by drawing lines to connect the paired words, ask students to write a sentence definition for each pair.

   Example:
   A garbunulent life style is a style of living that is frivolous, free, easy, and without heavy responsibilities.

   A sillory dignitary is a silly old man impressed with his own importance.

5. Suggest that pupils add their own nonsense social science combinations, using numbers 11-14, and create appropriate correlating definitions. The results will be fun to share!

6. Provide time for students to share their definitions and enjoy using the new words.

# DAFFY DEFINITIONS

Name _____

### Column I

1. garbunulent

2. quaqqled

3. cardoviar

4. bimulous

5. starrogatory

6. transvasculant

7. sillory

8. magnifoluscent

9. dusturious

10. mogumous

11. _____

12. _____

13. _____

14. _____

### Column II

city

life style

person

industry

government

means of transportation

geographical place

dignitary

law

map

_____

_____

_____

_____

Daffy-nitions:

1. _____

2. _____

3. _____

4. _____

5. _____

6. _____

7. _____

8. _____

9. _____

10. _____

## A DARING DOZEN

Purpose: After completing this activity the student should be able to demonstrate awareness of the strong contributions made by women to American social and political development.

1. Prepare a scrapbook of looseleaf pages which contains twelve sections—one for each of the following women:

   Abigail Adams                Julia Ward Howe
   Harriet Tubman               Eleanor Roosevelt
   Amelia Earhart               Dorothea Lynde Dix
   Susan B. Anthony             Sarah Jane Pittman
   Mary McLeon Bethune          Barbara Jordan
   Dolly Madison                Barbara Walters

2. Each section of this notebook should contain one or more pages for each of the following headings (the number used depends on the number of students who will use the notebook):

   I. Notes of Interest About Her Personal Life

   II. Life Experiences Which Shaped Her Character and Molded Her Values

   III. Formal and Informal Preparation for Her Historic Position (i.e., education, jobs, acquaintances, etc.)

   IV. Her Major Contributions to American Political and Social Welfare

   V. My Personal Opinion or Reaction to this Person

3. Ask students to choose at least two of the twelve women whom they will carefully research to make contributions to all five categories following those two names. They may add notes, drawings, comments, opinions, etc.

   Ask them to then choose at least two additional persons of the twelve about whom they will do some cursory reading and add comments to at least four more pages.

5. When the scrapbook has been completed, specify a time for students to read the book for information and enjoyment, and a further time when the information may be discussed by the class or by small groups of students.

Adaptations:

Names may be substituted for those in the list of a dozen.

Additional pages may be added for comments or for illustrations and other contributions.

The finished scrapbook may be added to the school or classroom library.

DO QUOTE ME, PLEASE

Purpose:     After completing this activity the student should be able
             to identify quotations of famous Americans and to place
             them in proper historical context.

1.    Reproduce copies of the work sheets on the following pages.  Cut
      each work sheet apart on the lines to make fourteen separate strips.

2.    Place the strips marked with "Q" in one envelope, the strips marked
      with "P" in another, and the strips marked with "O" in a third
      envelope.  (You should have as many envelopes as you have students,
      one-third with "Q" strips, one-third with "P" strips, and one-third
      with "O" strips.)  Mark the outside of each envelope with either
      "P", "Q", or "O".

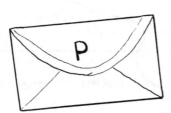 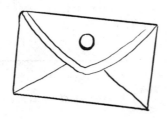 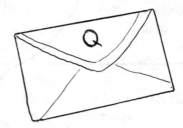

3.    Ask all students with "Q" envelopes to stand in one line, all with
      "P" envelopes in another, and all with "O" envelopes in a third.
      Tell them that the "Q" envelopes contain well-known quotes from
      famous people, the "P" envelopes contain the names of the persons
      quoted, and the "O" envelopes contain the time or occasion of the
      quote.  They are to form teams (one "P", one "Q", and one "O")
      to attempt to match the three.  Provide sheets of plain paper and
      paste to be used to rearrange the people, quotations, and dates in
      order.

      The first team to complete the assignment wins the game.

Adaptation and Extension:

Students may select one of the quotes to
research in detail and write a report on the
circumstances, or two quotations may be
selected as the basis for creative role-playing
(i.e., George Washington in conversation with
John Kennedy).

109

| | | |
|---|---|---|
| Revolutionary War | I have not yet begun to fight. | John Paul Jones |
| Revolutionary War Period | Give me liberty or give me death. | Patrick Henry |
| Man's first walk on the moon. | One small step for man, one giant step for mankind. | Neil Armstrong |
| Civil Rights Movement of the 1960s | I have a dream. | Martin Luther King |
| On 20th Century progress | Imagination is more important than knowledge. | Albert Einstein |
| From Poor Richard's Almanac – 18th Century | A penny saved is a penny earned. | Benjamin Franklin |
| Upon authorship of Uncle Tom's Cabin | I put my life's blood, my prayers, my tears into my book. | Harriett Beecher Stowe |

| | | |
|---|---|---|
| Early women's suffrage | A great world purpose cannot be achieved without women's participation and widest sympathy. | Jane Addams |
| Presidential Inaugural Address | Ask not what your country can do for you, but what you can do for your country. | John F. Kennedy |
| Early Space Exploration | We can lick gravity, but sometimes the paper work is overwhelming. | Werner Von Braun |
| Early 1900s | Genius is one percent inspiration and ninety-nine percent perspiration. | Thomas A. Edison |
| Revolutionary War Period | The nation which indulges toward another an habitual fondness is, in some degree, a slave. | George Washington |
| 20th Century | Rail-splitting produced an immortal president in Abraham Lincoln; but golf, with 29,000 courses, hasn't produced even a good A#1 congressman. | Will Rogers |
| Civil War Period | As I would not be a slave, so would I not be a master. This expresses my idea of a democracy. | Abraham Lincoln |

## HALL OF FAME

Purpose:     After completing this activity the student should be able
             to establish identification with heroes and heroines of
             the past.

1.   Provide a variety of biographical materials related to famous
     American men and women in both categories I and II from which
     students may choose one or more.  Give students a limited time
     in which to read their chosen materials.

2.   Distribute to each student a copy of the following page to use as
     a guide for preparing a Hall of Fame presentation.

3.   Create an area of special interest which may serve as a
     "museum-type" display area for final products.

I.  Choose a biography written about each of two famous American men or women.  Choose one from each of the following lists:

| List I | List II |
| --- | --- |
| a statesman or stateswoman | a writer |
| a leader | a poet |
| an inventor | an artist |
| a scientist | a musician |
| an explorer | an actor |
| a frontiersman or woman | an entertainer |
| a soldier | an athlete |

II.  Mark the following items to identify each person about whom you have read and his area of contribution or achievement.

I have chosen the following biographies:

List I:    Name _____

Area of Contribution or Achievement (circle one):

| | |
| --- | --- |
| Transportation | Religion |
| Communication | Conservation |
| Science | Human Welfare |
| Education | Military |
| Politics | Other _____ |

List II:    Name _____

Area of Contribution or Achievement (circle one):

| | |
| --- | --- |
| Art | Literature |
| Music | Sports |
| Drama | Other _____ |
| Theatre | |

III.  Read the two books you have chosen.  As you read think about the tasks required below so that you will be ready to do them.

IV.  For each of the two people you have read about, do the following things:

A.  Find or create an article of clothing this person might have worn.

B. Find or make an object that might have been a treasured belonging of this person.

C. Draw or trace his or her portrait or silhouette and frame it. (You may use a wood, paper, or metal frame.)

   Or draw a picture or diagram that tells about one of his or her achievements or contributions.

D. Make a small museum display on a board or in a box-- anything that may be used to display the above collection of items.

E. Add to your collection a small stand-up card that tells the person's name and how the things you have chosen represent this person and his or her life.

F. Place your collection in the Hall of Fame for others to use for learning and enjoyment!

# A HORSE IN THE HOUSE??

Purpose: After completing this activity the student should be able to identify with everyday life in the White House and its many famous occupants through acquaintance with two or more of the pets who have lived there.

1.  Give each student a copy of the following Study Starter.

2.  Ask them to use library reference materials to find answers to the "key" questions in Part I; then complete directed activities in Part II.

3.  Create a Pet Parade Center where students may place their completed products.

Name _____

A HORSE IN THE HOUSE?? – Study Starter

I.  Use your library to see if you can find out...

Which lady of the White House rode a horse up and down stairs?

_____

Who drove a herd of goats through the East Room of the White House?

_____

Which president kept a mockingbird for a pet?

_____

Which president's daughter had a pony named Macaroni?

_____

Which president was "Old Whitey's" master?

_____

To which famous occupants of the White House did these pets belong?

Fala_____

Macaw_____

Him and Her_____

Grits_____

II.    Choose a one-time White House pet and its master or mistress.

Draw a picture of the pet on a piece of heavy white construction paper or tagboard.

Cut out the picture and make a stand for it so it will stand up.

On the back of the picture write the name of the owner and a sentence that tells one funny or interesting thing about that pet.

Place your finished product in the Pet Parade Center for others to enjoy.

OWNER:
ULYSSES S. GRANT

THIS WAS HIS FAVORITE HORSE TO RIDE DURING THE CIVIL WAR. THE HORSE'S NAME IS CINCINNATI, AND HE IS A HUGE BLACK CHARGER.

# IS YOUR CONGRESS MEMBER ALIVE AND WELL?

| Purpose: | After completing this activity the student should be able to interpret and react to the role of congress member. |
|---|---|

1. Provide varied resources dealing with the election procedures, role, and responsibilities of congress members.

2. Ask students to read, interview adults, work in peer groups, or view films to gain information to complete the questionnaire on the following page.

3. Arrange for a follow-up discussion for sharing the completed study sheets.

4. Ask each student to write a letter to one of his congress members to indicate direction he feels should be taken on a contemporary issue of social consequence.

5. Appoint a student committee to collect and mail the letters.

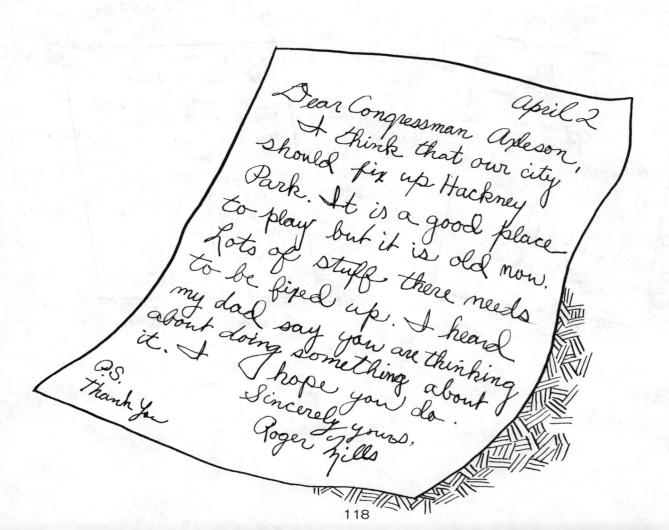

Dear Congressman Axleson,

April 2

I think that our city should fix up Hackney Park. It is a good place to play but it is old now. Lots of stuff there needs to be fixed up. I heard my dad say you are thinking about doing something about it. I hope you do.

Sincerely yours,
Roger Mills

P.S.
Thank You

# INFORMATION SHEET

Full name of congress member _____

What state or district is represented? _____

Washington address: _____

_____

Home address: _____

_____

Is the congress member a member of the Senate or of the House of Representatives? _____

Age _____ Marital Status _____

Occupation (before Congress) _____

Educational background _____

_____

Current issue before congress _____

_____

Congress member's stand on the issue _____

_____

Major issues of Congress member's campaign _____

_____

Platform _____

_____

Notes of interest about Congress member's record _____

_____

# IT'S WHAT'S ON TOP THAT COUNTS!

Purpose: After completing this activity the student should be able to demonstrate his awareness of the many American traditions, events, and holidays.

1. Provide for the students varied resources dealing with American traditions, events, and holidays (see Bibliography). Ask students to read, interview adults, and check with additional library resources to identify at least ten holidays or special events traditionally celebrated in the United States.

2. Provide for each student a heavy piece of tagboard or construction paper on which these days may be noted in the following manner:

| Name of Holiday | Date | Purpose/Origin | Traditional Activity for Celebration |
|---|---|---|---|
| 1. | | | |
| 2. | | | |
| 3. | | | |

3.  Have the student complete his list and choose from it one holiday with which he was not previously familiar.  Using scraps from the classroom art supply and lots of imagination, he must create a holiday hat which might be worn in celebration of the event he has chosen.

4.  Encourage students to make their hats as unique and creative and as suggestive of the "feeling" of that holiday's origin and purpose as possible.

5.  Provide a time for students to model their hats and share the important facts surrounding their chosen events.

Adaptation:

On a special day designated as a "ME AND MY WORLD DAY", each student might create a "personality" hat which depicts his perception of himself—his likes, his ideas, what's important to him, etc.

# LANDSCAPE LINGO

Purpose:   After completing this activity the student should be able to identify and describe the major geographical land forms.

1. Provide black and red markers, unlabeled maps, and the list of terms (found on the following pages) for each student.

2. Use the unlabeled map following this page as a model to present an enlarged panorama of land forms to students. (Do this by using an opaque projector, using the page to make an overhead transparency, or copying the map on a large poster or bulletin board.)

3. Ask students to work with you in identifying the various items you wish to identify. (Let them label at random those they already know. Then present the terms less familiar and let them try to identify them.)

4. Attempt to define or describe each term as you proceed.

5. Give each student a copy of the unlabeled map and a list of the terms defined after the large map has been labeled satisfactorily. (You might star the required terms and leave others to be identified as an optional activity.) The large map may or may not be left in view.

6. Ask the student to locate and label as many of the required items as possible on his map.

7. When he has finished, he may check his map with the large map to find errors and fill in those he could not do.

8. Allow students to keep maps for study purposes.

9. Provide students with another copy of the unlabeled map at a later date to use as a self-test.

Adaptation:

Students might use map to create an identical relief sandbox or salt map which may then be labeled with flags and used as a manipulative learning device for practice in identifying geographical terms.

Geographical terms for you to know:

| | | |
|---|---|---|
| sea | dock | dormant volcano |
| gulf | pier | crater |
| harbor | wharf | piedmont |
| bay | road | slope |
| shoal | field | gorge |
| reef | meadow | ridge |
| channel | pasture | divide |
| strait | highway | lake |
| sound | grove | river |
| fjord | timber | pond |
| inlet | timber line | stream |
| delta | canyon | brook |
| breakwater | forest | waterfall |
| island | foothills | river mouth |
| cape | summit | reservoir |
| peninsula | peak | dam |
| sand bar | mountain range | dune |
| beach | plateau | mesa |
| shore line | valley | desert |
| seaport | hill | oasis |
| | active volcano | |

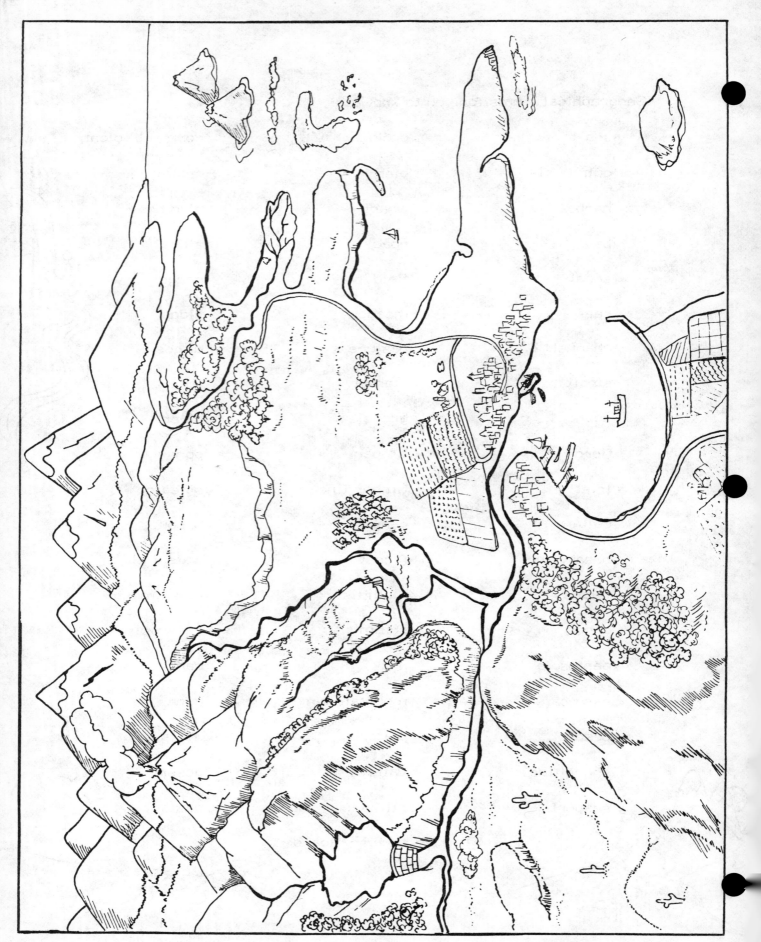

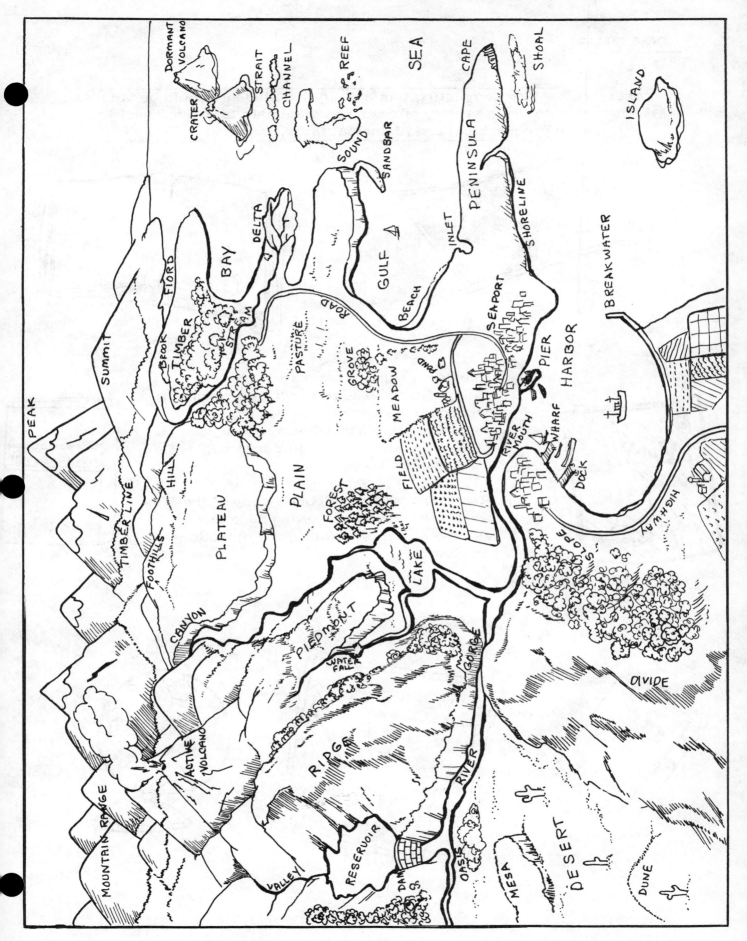

PEAK · SUMMIT · MOUNTAIN RANGE · TIMBER LINE · FOOTHILLS · HILL · BROOK · FIORD · TIMBER · STREAM · BAY · DELTA · CRATER · DORMANT VOLCANO · STRAIT · CHANNEL · REEF · GULF · SOUND · SANDBAR · SEA · CAPE · SHOAL · PENINSULA · SHORELINE · INLET · BEACH · ISLAND · BREAKWATER · PLATEAU · PLAIN · PASTURE · ROAD · FOREST · GROVE · MEADOW · FIELD · POND · SEAPORT · PIER · WHARF · HARBOR · RIVER MOUTH · DOCK · HIGHWAY · CANYON · PIEDMONT · LAKE · WATER FALL · RIDGE · GORGE · DIVIDE · ACTIVE VOLCANO · VALLEY · RESERVOIR · DAM · RIVER · OASIS · MESA · DESERT · DUNE

125

## LOOK IT UP!

Purpose: After completing this activity the student should be able to use a variety of resource materials to locate specific geographical and historical facts.

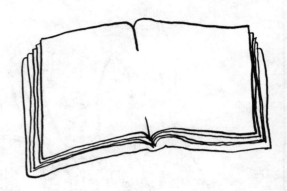

1.  Provide a copy of the map of the United States (see Appendix) for each student and a variety of resource materials, including flat maps, a globe, encyclopedias, dictionaries, atlases, and textbooks.

2.  Reproduce and distribute a copy of the work sheet on the following page and ask the students to follow the directions as given.

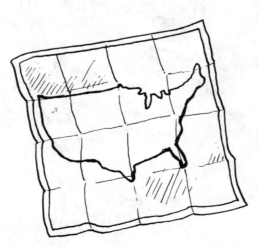

LOOK IT UP! – Work Sheet

Use the appropriate resource materials to find the information you need to follow the directions given on this page. Write the source used in the box beside each number.

1. [                                    ]

Circle the largest and smallest states with your black crayon. Write the names and one interesting fact about each state on the back of the map.

2. [                                    ]

Color the northern region of the United States green, the southern region orange, the western region brown, and the eastern region blue.

3. [                                    ]

Draw a picture of the state flower of one state from each of the four regions on the back of the map. Label each flower.

4. [                                    ]

Locate and mark with "R" all the major rivers.

5. [                                    ]

Locate and mark with "D" all the major desert areas.

6. [                                    ]

Locate and mark with "M" all major mountain areas.

7. [                                    ]

Mark a red "X" on each of the thirteen original states. Print the names of these states on the back of the map and draw a picture of the flag adopted by these states.

8. [                                    ]

Draw boxes around the last two states admitted to the Union. Write the names and chief industries of each on the back of the map.

9. [                                    ]

Plan a trip you'd like to take. Chart it on the map with your purple crayon.

Use your own paper to design a travel poster or Chamber of Commerce brochure for the state you selected to visit (similar to the ones below).  Use your crayons and felt tip pens to make it as colorful and attractive as possible, and use the resource materials to gather accurate information.

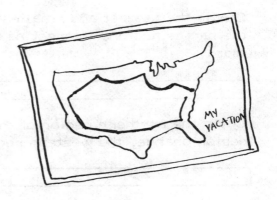

## MADE IN AMERICA

Purpose: After completing this activity the student should be able to identify with both the early American Indian culture and the life styles of today's American Indians.

1. Provide a large variety of reference and resource materials related to American Indians. Place these where students may use them freely.

2. Prepare the following pages so that each student may have one of his own to use as a study guide.

3. Ask students to follow instructions on the study guide to complete the directed activities.

A Comparison of

Early American Indians          and          Indians of America Today

Use as many resource books and materials as possible to find facts about Early American Indians and Indians of America Today. Then complete the following activities.

I.  For each topic listed below, write one thing that is the same about the two groups of Indians and one thing that has changed.

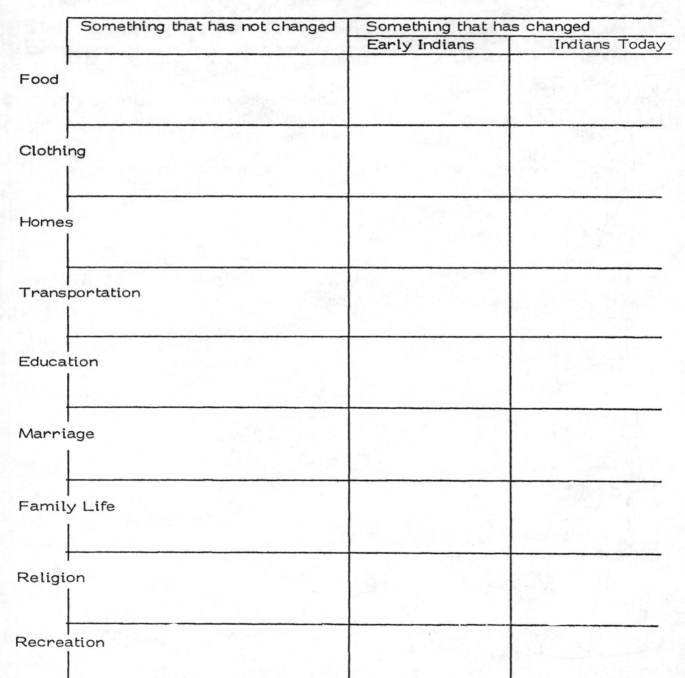

| | Something that has not changed | Something that has changed | |
| --- | --- | --- | --- |
| | | Early Indians | Indians Today |
| Food | | | |
| Clothing | | | |
| Homes | | | |
| Transportation | | | |
| Education | | | |
| Marriage | | | |
| Family Life | | | |
| Religion | | | |
| Recreation | | | |

II. Use reference materials to find out about the words in the following list. Beside each word write a sentence that tells about the word or draw a small picture that illustrates its meaning.

Happy Hunting Ground

Peace Pipe

Sand Painting

Trading Post

Wampum

Indian Removal Act

Moccasin

Cliff Dwellers

Sacagawea

Crazy Horse

Sitting Bull

Red Power

Hogan

Snake Dance

Bureau of Indian Affairs

131

III. Name at least three things the white man has learned from the Indian that has made America a better place to live today.

A. _____
_____
_____

B. _____
_____
_____

C. _____
_____
_____

IV. Choose one special thing that interests you about Indian life either long ago or today. Use your own paper to write a poem or song,

or

find a collection of Indian legends and stories. Choose one to read and use the space below or another piece of paper to draw your impressions about the legend.

# MEDIA SURVEY

Purpose: After completing this activity the student should be familiar with at least four of the news media and explain the role and impact of each upon the "public ear".

1. Choose a news item of national significance which will likely be noted by all of the news media.

2. Attempt to find a television or radio news broadcast which mentions this item for the entire class to watch or hear together.

3. Ask students to read about the same incident in a local newspaper and in at least one news magazine, i.e., Time, Newsweek, U. S. News & World Report. Also they should attempt to hear it mentioned on one additional television or radio broadcast (on a station other than the one listened to in class).

4. Students should be prepared to evaluate what they have heard and seen and be ready to express an opinion about which news media presented the items (1) most completely (best coverage), (2) most objectively (with least bias), and (3) most attractively (got your attention best).

5. Ask students to repeat the entire process with yet another news item (of their choice) to see if their original conclusions can be reinforced.

6. Provide time for discussion of ways in which the various media influence the public; how ownership of a newspaper, magazine, television, or radio station might influence news content and presentation.

## MONEY BUSINESS

Purpose: After completing this activity the student should be able to explain people's need for money, how they get it, and things that can be done with money.

1.  Duplicate the following pages so each student may have his own BOOK ABOUT MONEY. Give each student a blank page on which he may make a cover and write his own title.

2.  Use the booklet as is fitting for your students' ages and ability levels.

3.  Additional pages may be added for practice in counting or using money.

People need money for many things. These pictures show some of the things that money can buy. Can you tell about them?

_____

_____

_____

_____

_____

_____

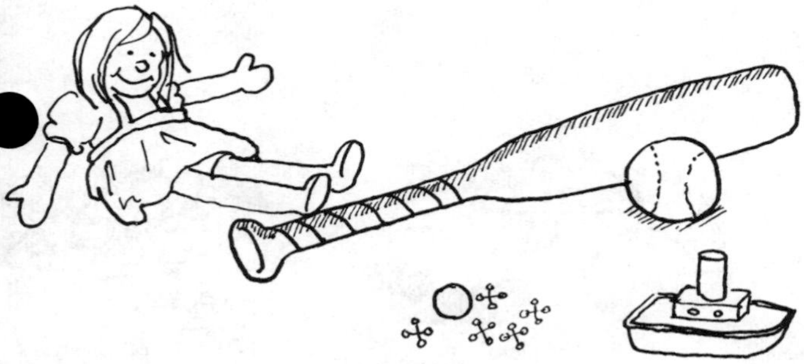

_____

_____

_____

_____

_____

_____

_____

_____

_____

How do people get money?

By working to earn it:

What work does each of these people do to earn money?

_____  _____  _____  _____

By selling or renting things they have:

By lending money to other people:

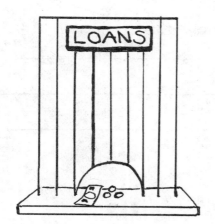

(The money they receive for lending their money is called <u>interest</u>. Lending money is called <u>investing</u>.)

What happens to money you spend at the store? Does the store owner get to keep it all?

This is what he does with it. Can you write or tell about it?

He buys things to sell.

He hires people to help him.

He pays for his building.

He pays for utilities.

He pays taxes and insurance.

He pays the bank any money he has borrowed.

He gets to keep what is left.

What he keeps is called his profit or income.

Write the word that tells what he keeps. _____

Name _____

Most people try to save some of their money in case they have an emergency or need something special.

Boys and girls can start to save while they are young.  The best way to save is to take some money away from each little bit you get or earn and put it in a bank.

You might keep                                                        it in a safe place at
home.  Or you                                                       might take it to a bank
and deposit it.

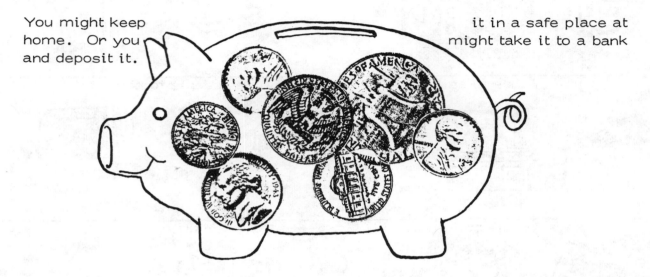

How much money has the owner of this piggy bank saved? _____ ¢

When you take money to a bank, the bank gives you a book or a paper that tells how much money it keeps for you.

| | DATE | WITHDRAWALS | CREDITS | EARNINGS | BALANCE | TRANS. |
|---|---|---|---|---|---|---|
| 1 | 12-04-68 | | | | | |
| 2 | 12-24-68 | | 273.60 | | | |
| 3 | 1-17-69 | | | 1.02 | 273.60 | 38A |
| 4 | 3-03-69 | | 144.34 | | 274.62 | |
| 5 | 4-04-69 | | 121.11 | | 418.96 | 38B |
| 6 | 5-05-69 | | 63.44 | | 540.07 | 38B |
| 7 | 6-25-69 | | 374.00 | | 603.51 | 38B |
| 8 | 7-09-69 | 500.00 | | 14.19 | 977.51 | 38A |
| 9 | 8-15-69 | 250.00 | | | 991.70 | |
| | | | | | 491.70 | 38A |
| | | | | | 241.70 | 38A |

No. M 20184

How much money has been saved by the owner of this deposit book?

_____ ¢

Name _____

Make a picture of something for which you would like to save your money.
Write a sentence under the picture that tells why you would like to have this.

## THE NUMBERS GAME

Purpose:    After completing this activity the student should be able
to relate the purpose and use of certain kinds of
identification numbers common to the American way
of life.

1.   Show students a collection
     of credit cards, licenses, identi-
     fication cards, etc. that bear
     identification numbers.

2.   Ask them to conjecture what
     meaning the numbers might
     have for the distributor.

3.   Write a social security number
     on the board.  Discuss what a
     social security number is, why
     one is needed, how one is
     obtained, and the purposes for
     which it is most often used.

4.   Make a list of kinds of numbers that
     may be investigated by students to
     increase their understanding of the use of
     numbers for identification, organization,
     and economic control, such as:

     social security number                    membership card number
     department store credit card number       driver's license number
     gasoline company credit card number       zip code number
     bank identification card number           phone area code number
     job identification card number            military service number

5.   Appoint a small group of students to investigate one of each type of
     number on the list.  They should try to find out:

     (1) what each part of the number stands for
     (2) how each is used by its distributor
     (3) other uses for the number by the owner
     (4) advantages of being the owner of this type card or number
     (5) disadvantages of being the owner of this type card or number

# ON THE SHIPSIDE

Purpose: After completing this activity the student should be able to demonstrate his understanding of the role played by transportation in the history and development of the United States.

1.  Provide either a copy of the pictured ships for each student, or place an enlargement of the same where all students may have access to it.

2.  Give each student a copy of the Students' Study Guide to Boats and Ships and review the required tasks and resource possibilities.

3.  Ask each student to complete his own study and provide some basis for sharing and evaluation.

4.  Provide a variety of resource materials pertaining to ships and vessels identified with the development of United States land and industry (see Bibliography).

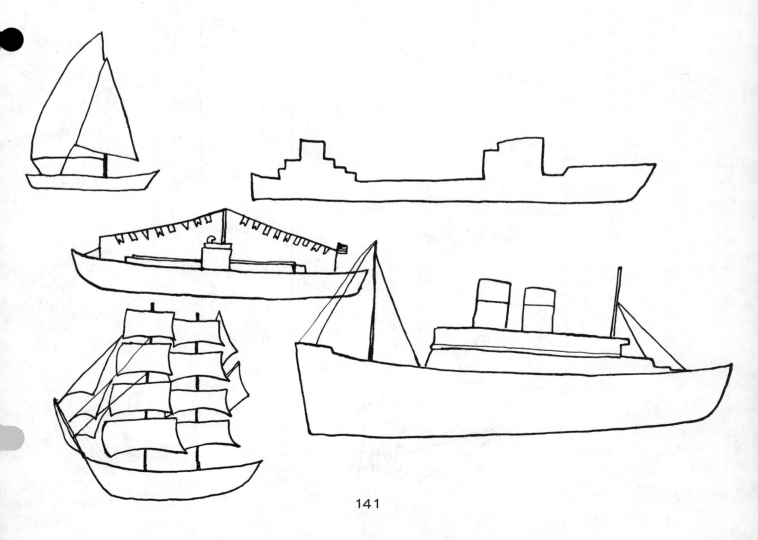

STUDENTS' STUDY GUIDE TO BOATS AND SHIPS

A. Choose at least three of the pictured boats and ships and use all possible resources to provide the following information about each:

| | I | II | III |
|---|---|---|---|
| Name or kind of vessel | | | |
| Special function (use) | | | |
| Geographical area where most often used | | | |
| Short paragraph describing how this vessel might have helped in development of United States land or industry | | | |
| Identify a story—fact or fiction—in which this type of vessel appears | | | |

B. Write a brief description of a typical day spent as the captain, owner, or crewman of this type of vessel. (Optional: Draw or trace a picture on a separate sheet of paper to accompany your story.)

142

SHOW BOAT

# OUR COUNTRY'S FLOWER GARDEN

Purpose: | After completing this activity the student should be able to identify the state flowers of the fifty United States.

1.  Provide reference books with colored pictures of the state flowers of each of the fifty United States, sheets of onionskin paper, felt tip pens, glue, pencils, scissors, multi-color tissue paper, and an old double-bed sized sheet.

2.  Use a permanent felt tip pen to section the sheet into fifty squares.

3.  Ask the students to research the flowers designated as state flowers. Assign one or more flowers to each student to reproduce according to the following directions:

    (1)  Draw the state flower in outline form (including leaves and stems) on one sheet of onionskin.

    (2)  Fill in the outline with appropriately colored paper torn into small pieces and pasted on. Use felt tip pens as needed to provide details for the flowers.

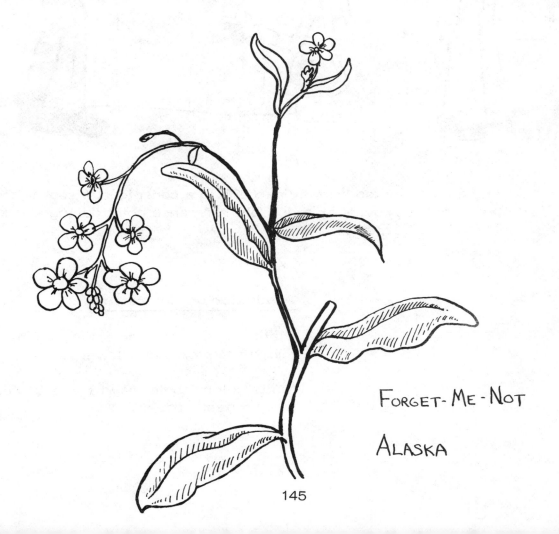

FORGET-ME-NOT

ALASKA

3. Allow the paste to dry thoroughly and cut the flower out.

4. Paste one cut-out tissue paper flower inside each "box" on the sheet and use a felt tip pen to label the box with the name of the flower and the state it represents.

5. Hang the completed "flower garden" in a conspicuous spot in the classroom to provide an enjoyable reference point during a study of the United States.

Adaptation or Extension:

State flags, birds, or seals may be substituted for state flowers.

Multi-color fabric may be substituted for the tissue paper.

146

# SILENT NAMESAKES

Purpose:    After completing this activity the student should be able to cite examples and explain origins of the names of public places.

1.   On the chalk board make a partial list of buildings, streets, stadiums, parks, etc. in your area which have been named after important people.

   Examples:          Eisenhower Expressway
                      Cape Kennedy
                      Goethals Bridge
                      Rickenbacker Causeway
                      Percy Warner Park
                      Stahlman Auditorium

2.   Read the list aloud to students and ask them to offer additions.  Try to make the list long enough to provide one item for each student or pair of students in the class.  (Places of national fame or significance may be added to round out the list, i.e., Cape Kennedy.)

3.   Assign or allow each student or pair of students to choose one place on the list.

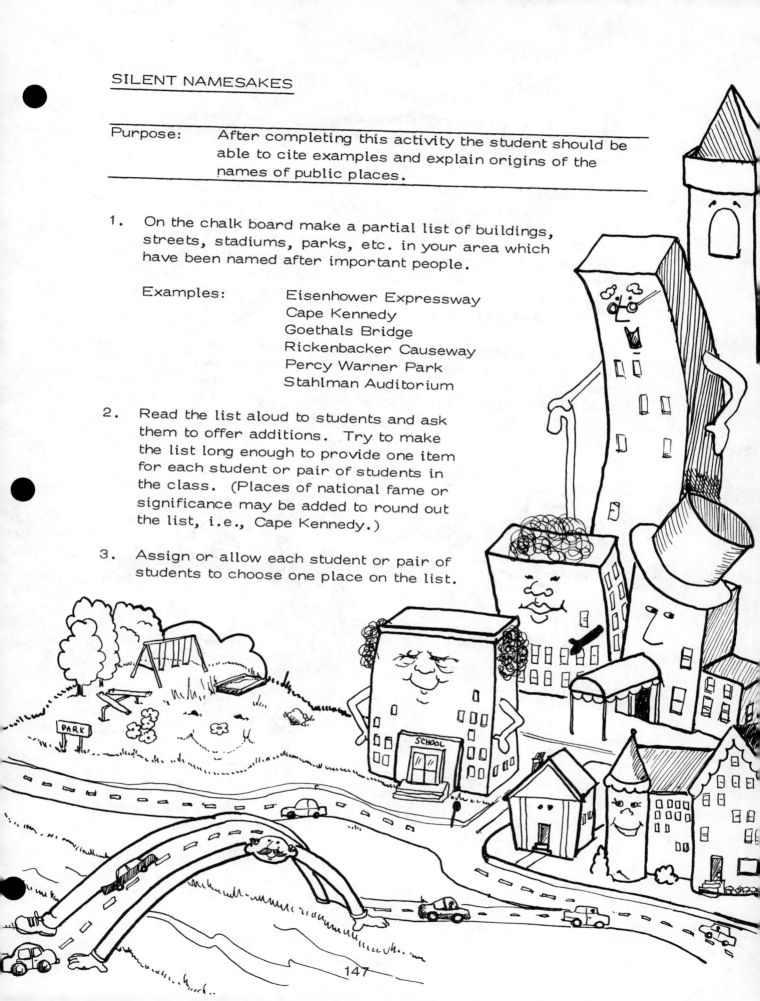

147

4.  Ask students to research the naming of their chosen place to determine why and how the name was chosen, by whom, what ceremony, if any, was involved, etc.

5.   Have students then create either a drawing or simple replica and a brief accompanying biography (either written to be read aloud to the class or tape recorded to be played for the class).  The biography should be composed in first person, i.e., "I am Cape Kennedy.  I formerly was Cape Canaveral, but upon the death of John F. Kennedy, who was the 35th president of the United States and whose interests were very much directed toward development of the United States space program, I was renamed Cape Kennedy, etc.".

6.  When all replicas, drawings, and biographies have been completed, appoint a V.I.P. (Very Important Place) Day.  Ask each student or pair of students to make an appropriate presentation.  Create an observation area in the classroom where these projects may be revisited in the students' spare time for several days.

## A STATE IS BORN

Purpose: | After completing this activity the student should be able to relate to important facts and events in the early historic development of his home state.

1.  Prepare the following Investigation Guide for student use in discovering information about the early history of his home state by superimposing an outline silhouette of the state on top of the written page. (This may be done by tracing an outline of the state directly upon the Investigation Guide page in black felt tip pen so that the page appears similar to the following:

2.  Provide a copy of this guide page to each student.

3.  Provide a variety of resource texts and materials from which students may gain information about the early history of the state.

4.  Cut from large, heavy tag or corrugated board a three to five foot shape of the state. Make it colorful and attractive by painting it or covering it with colored contact paper or a collage effect of cut pictures representative of the state history, geography, climate, occupations, resources, etc.

5.  Hang this shape in a position horizontal to the ceiling and attach a number of strings which hang down from the shape in the fashion shown here to form a mobile.

6.  Direct students to use the Investigation Guide sheet to collect information related to the early history of the state.

7.  Provide each student with a piece of tagboard approximately 5 x 7" in size after he has completed his guide sheet.

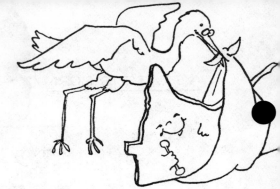

A STATE IS BORN – Investigation Guide

1.    The name of my state is _____.

2.    In earlier days the area where this state is now located may have been
called _____

_____

3.    The year when people began to settle in this state was _____

4.    Some of the reasons they came to this state to settle are:

_____

_____

_____

5.    Here are some of the ways early settlers in this state traveled:

_____

_____

6.    In order to earn a living, these early state settlers _____

_____

_____

_____

7.    Below are the names of five places in this state for which I have
discovered the origin:

        Name of Place                    How It Got Its Name

(1) _____       _____

                                               _____

(2) _____       _____

                                               _____

(3) _____     _____

_____

(4) _____     _____

_____

(5) _____     _____

_____

8.    This state was important in the founding and development of our nation because

_____

_____

_____

_____

9.    Places of special historical interest in this state are:

_____

_____

_____

_____

10.    Some famous personalities (inventors, scientists, discoverers, entertainers, statesmen, sportsmen, etc.) from the past history of this state are:

_____

_____

_____

_____

8.    Have the student write on one side of this card one significant fact he has learned about the early history of his state.

On the other side he should draw or paste a picture that tells something about the early history of his state.

9.    Instruct the student to use a paper punch to make a hole at the top of his card when this task has been completed, and tie the card to one of the available strings on the mobile.

10.    Have facts and pictures shared by the group as a whole in a culmination or summary session at a later time.

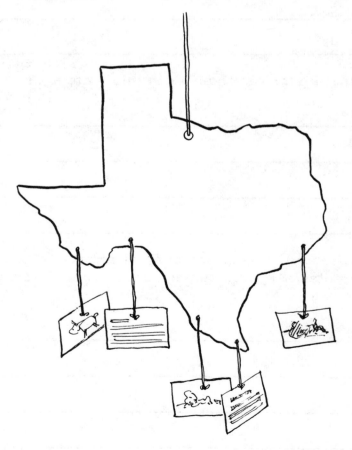

# STEP-A-MILE

**Purpose:** After completing this activity the student should be able to demonstrate his understanding of the directions north, south, east, and west and the mile as a measure of distance.

1. Clear a large area of floor space or outdoor playground space where the following map may be drawn with strips of tape or with chalk lines:

2. Add the symbols for north, south, east, and west.

3. Introduce the map to the students by standing at the south side of the map, looking north and identifying with them the directions and the map symbols for ocean, forest, mountains, and lakes.

4. Ask a student to stand in the center of the map. Tell him that we will pretend that each of his feet is a mile long. When he takes one step he has traveled one mile; when he has taken two steps he has traveled two miles, etc.

5. Ask the student to face north. Then give instructions similar to the following:

   (1) Go two miles to the north.

   (2) Go two miles to the east.

   (3) Go five miles from there toward the mountains.

   (4) What direction did you go to get to the mountains?

6. Ask each student, in turn, to take a given place on the map and proceed with similar instructions until all students seem to have a "good feel" of directions and using symbols.

Adaptations:

1. The activity may be played in teams--the team making the most correct moves wins.

2. The activity may be used as a math game, counting miles, and adding and subtracting distances.

## STEP RIGHT UP, FOLKS

| Purpose: | After completing this activity the student should be able to creatively express awareness of the influence of printed advertising on consumer buying. |

1.  Ask students to contribute to a collection of mail order catalogs, yellow pages from old telephone directories, newspapers, and other printed materials devoted to advertising.

2.  Use the collection to initiate a discussion of the influence of printed advertising on consumer purchasing.  Encourage students to draw on experiences within their own families related to decisions to purchase items on the basis of printed advertising.  Ask questions such as "Did the advertising cause you to want to own the item, or did you want it first and then look at the ads for information as to where and how to get the best buy?", or "Was the information in the ad accurate or misleading?"

    Discuss the cost of advertising and lead students to question the addition of this cost to the price of the merchandise and in turn to its actual worth to the consumer.

3.  Ask each student to select one ad from the materials collection to analyze as the discussion continues.  Distribute copies of the work sheet on the following page to facilitate lively discussion and total class involvement.

4.  Culminate the discussion by creating a new product to be presented to the public for the first time through an advertising campaign to be developed by the group.  For example:

    a synthetic fabric designed to retain heat in
    cold weather and to repel heat in warm weather

    a pill containing all the food value needed for
    twenty-four hours

5.  Distribute newsprint or manila paper, felt tip pens, and dictionaries. Instruct each student to design the very best ad possible to introduce the new product.  Discuss the influence of a catchy name, a slogan, logo, word usage in the content of the ad, graphics, and total space usage.

6.   Provide time for each ad to be evaluated by the group before being placed on a bulletin board or other display area to stimulate further discussion.

Extension or Adaptation:

For more mature students plan learning experiences to span several days and add one or more of the following activities:

(1)  Add product packaging materials to the media collection and discuss advertising strategy involved in package development, i.e., detergent boxes, candy bar wrappers, cosmetic containers, record jackets, etc.  Use the basic format of the discussion work sheet in evaluating the psychological effectiveness of the package on the intended buyer. Ask the students to design a container for the new product (including all printing and graphics on the container).

(2)  Plan a field trip to a grocery or department store to study packaging techniques. Instruct each student to select one "good" package and one "poor" package and to explain the basis for his decision.

(3)  Invite a resource person from a local advertising agency to talk to the class about the world of advertising, including the various steps involved in selling, conceiving and developing ads, relative costs, and the kinds of talents and academic preparation necessary for various careers in advertising

(4)  Involve the class in planning a radio and television campaign to accompany the printed advertising.

For younger or less able students limit the class discussion to ways in which consumer buying is influenced by advertising.  Simplify or omit the work sheet and focus attention on creative project development.

STEP RIGHT UP, FOLKS – Work Sheet

1.     Product advertised _____

_____

2.     Ad found in _____

_____

3.     Date of ad _____

4.     What audience is the ad directed to (men, women, children, teenagers, etc.)?

_____

5.     How accurately is the product described? _____

_____

6.     List some sales promotion words (i.e., deluxe, super, special, bonus, etc.)

_____

_____

7.     What kind of appeal is being made to the buyer (get smart, grab a bargain, select quality, etc.)?

_____

_____

8.     How well does the art work contribute to the effectiveness of the ad?

_____

9.     Is all the space well used? _____

10.    What is your overall evaluation of the effect of this ad on the consumer?

_____

# SYMBOLS SAY A LOT!

Purpose: After completing this activity the student should be able to demonstrate understanding of the symbols of our country as representative of things, events, and feelings that are important to a people.

1. Present the following page to the students.

2. Discuss the symbols of the United States:

   flag                                    Pledge of Allegiance
   seal                                    eagle
                    National Anthem

   What meaning does each part, picture, word, etc. have? (Someone might have previously been assigned to research each one and tell about its origin, etc.)

3. Provide a variety of art materials and scraps. Ask students to complete the student page and make arrangements for sharing resulting products and ideas at a later time or in a specific area of the classroom.

Adaptation:

The entire class or small groups of students might work together on the assignment rather than asking each individual to do his own.

These are pictures of several of the symbols that represent the thoughts, ideas, events, and values that are important to the people of the United States. Try to figure out how and why these particular symbols were created. What does each part of the symbol mean? Notice how words and picture symbols are used together to create the Great Seal of the United States. In the space below, design a badge, flag, or seal, or write a song or poem that presents the things about America of which you are proud.

# TAX-ONOMY (TAX-ON-A-ME!)

**Purpose:** After completing this activity the student should be able to perform the basic tasks involved in filing a United States income tax form.

1. Secure the latest federal income tax forms and illustrated instruction booklet from the nearest bank or Internal Revenue Service office.

2. Discuss with the students the concept of income tax and the American government's pattern of operation in taxing a citizen's income. Discuss terms such as "deductions", "interest", and any other words on the forms that students may not know.

3. Supply one form for each student and ask them to use the following information sheet to complete and file income tax information for the A. Merican family.

4. Provide for short periods of time to hold "tax forum" for the purpose of answering questions as they arise and offering assistance.

5. When forms have been completed, compare and check answers. Also it might be interesting to consider some weighty questions such as:

   (1) Do you think our federal income tax system is fair to <u>all</u> taxpayers?

   (2) Do you think our taxes are <u>high</u> or low for the conveniences and privileges Americans enjoy?

   (3) How does our tax system compare to those of other countries around the world?

# TAX INFORMATION SHEET

Use the information below to complete a federal income tax form.

> Mr. A. Merican and wife, Ima Merican, are each 41 years old.
> They have two children: son (16 years old), and daughter (12 years old).
>
> Mr. Merican is an insurance agent. He and his family live in a 10-room house. One room of this house is Mr. Merican's business office.
>
> For this tax year he earned a salary of $19,500 from his insurance business. He earned additional income of $1,400 royalties paid on a handbook he wrote on insurance buying. His wife, Ima, earned $4,200 as a dance instructor. Together they paid property tax of $1,280 and state income tax to the State of New York totaling $900. They make a monthly mortgage payment on their home of $267. $190 of this payment is interest.
>
> This tax year they bought a new car for which they pay $110 a month. $36 per month of this payment is interest.
>
> Mr. A. Merican traveled 8,000 miles for his business and another 7,000 miles for pleasure. He spent $540 on business entertainment. The family had no medical expenses.

Using this information and the latest federal income tax form and illustrated booklet, figure how much Mr. and Mrs. A. Merican owe the Internal Revenue Service. Keep a list of difficult words and instructions you do not understand. Your teacher will provide short "tax forums" or times when you may ask for information or assistance.

TELL-TALE TRASH

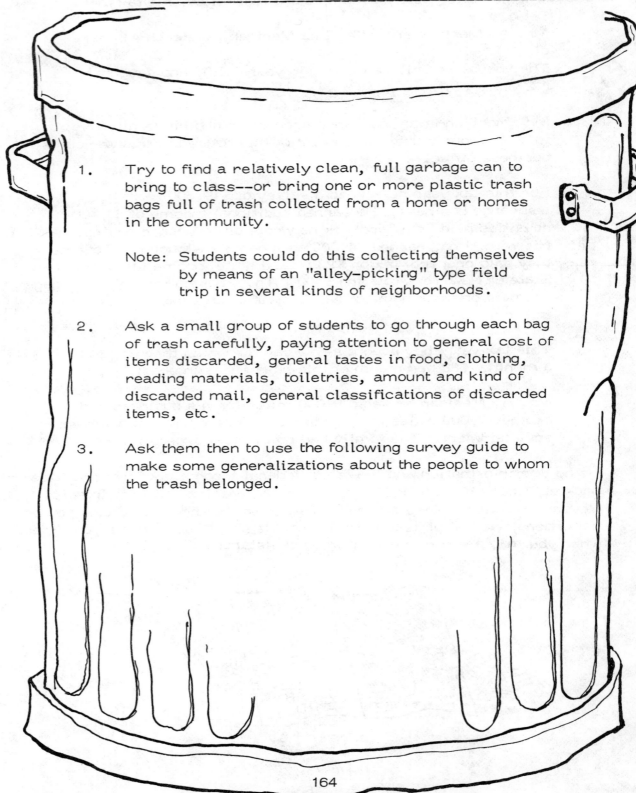

Purpose: After completing this activity the student should be able to demonstrate progress in intuitive and deductive thinking and should be able to relate a person's economic status to his life style.

1. Try to find a relatively clean, full garbage can to bring to class--or bring one or more plastic trash bags full of trash collected from a home or homes in the community.

   Note: Students could do this collecting themselves by means of an "alley-picking" type field trip in several kinds of neighborhoods.

2. Ask a small group of students to go through each bag of trash carefully, paying attention to general cost of items discarded, general tastes in food, clothing, reading materials, toiletries, amount and kind of discarded mail, general classifications of discarded items, etc.

3. Ask them then to use the following survey guide to make some generalizations about the people to whom the trash belonged.

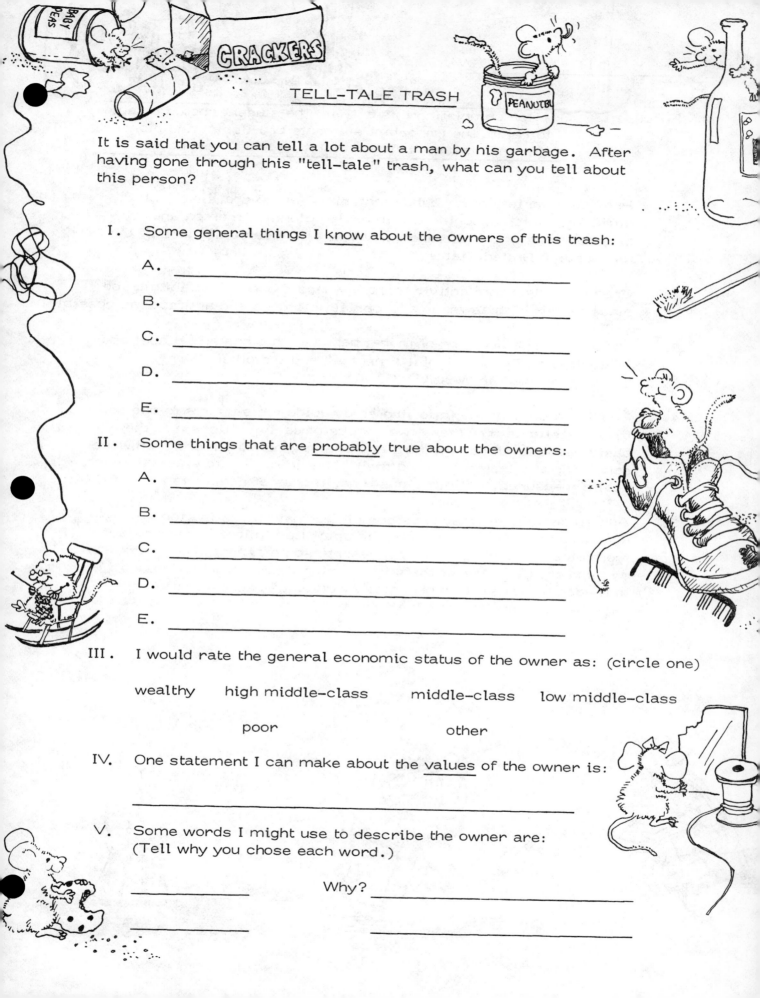

TELL-TALE TRASH

It is said that you can tell a lot about a man by his garbage.  After having gone through this "tell-tale" trash, what can you tell about this person?

I.   Some general things I <u>know</u> about the owners of this trash:

A. _____

B. _____

C. _____

D. _____

E. _____

II.  Some things that are <u>probably</u> true about the owners:

A. _____

B. _____

C. _____

D. _____

E. _____

III. I would rate the general economic status of the owner as:  (circle one)

wealthy      high middle-class      middle-class      low middle-class

poor                              other

IV.  One statement I can make about the <u>values</u> of the owner is:

_____

V.   Some words I might use to describe the owner are:
(Tell why you chose each word.)

_____        Why? _____

_____                _____

## THEY DID IT THE HARD WAY

**Purpose:**  After completing this activity the student should be able to relate the important elements of Pilgrim and pioneer life and discuss their similarities and differences.

1.  Provide a variety of resource materials (at several levels of difficulty) which describe life in early colonial America and give accounts of the life and activities of the early settlers of the far western United States.

2.  Create a classroom activity center where these materials may be placed along with as many appropriate pictures and artifacts as possible.

3.  Hang two large sections of mural paper at this center.  Label one "Pilgrims of Early Colonial America" and the other "Early Settlers of the Far West".

4.  Provide a copy of the following study guide for students to use as they investigate how these two groups of early settlers met their basic needs for food, clothing and shelter; how their children were schooled; how they conducted their lives in regard to entertainment, health measures, religious customs, modes of dress, family life, etc.

5.  Ask students when they have completed their investigations to add to each mural at least one pictorial item (either drawn or cut from other material) which represents some aspect of Pilgrim or pioneer life.  Assist them in planning these contributions so that each mural section becomes a "collage" representation of early American life.

## THEY DID IT THE HARD WAY – Study Guide

Consult all available resource materials to find information about life in early colonial and western pioneer days. Use this guide to help you list important facts about each group of settlers and make comparisons between the two groups.

|  | PILGRIMS OF EARLY COLONIAL AMERICA | EARLY SETTLERS OF THE FAR WEST |
|---|---|---|
| Most common foods |  |  |
| Source of foods |  |  |
| Typical dress for male |  |  |
| Typical dress for female |  |  |
| Kinds of homes |  |  |
| Resources used for building homes |  |  |
| How children were educated |  |  |

| | |
|---|---|
| What they did for fun and entertainment: | |
| Adults | |
| Children | |
| Health problems and solutions | |
| Religious beliefs and practices | |
| Choose one person from each group who made a strong contribution to his or her community. | |
| Write a short paragraph describing this person and telling why he or she was important. | |

THEY EYE WHAT YOU EAT!

Purpose: After completing this activity the student should be able to describe the function of the United States Food and Drug Administration and relate specific steps taken by that agency to protect American life and health.

1.   Gather as many resource materials as possible related to the United States Food and Drug Administration. (Numerous pamphlets, brochures, etc. may be obtained by writing this agency at the Office of Public Affairs, 5600 Fishers Lane, Rockville, Maryland 20852 or by contacting state health departments. See Bibliography for additional resources.) If possible, invite a resource person who works for the FDA to visit the class or set up an interview by phone and tape record it!

2.   Assign to each student one of the following roles:

         Consumer safety officer of the FDA
         FDA laboratory scientist
         FDA researcher
         FDA food inspector
         FDA drug inspector

3.   Ask him to check reference and resource materials and/or correspond with or call the HEW, FDA, or state health department, or interview a person employed by one of these agencies.

4.   The student should keep a list of every job that is done by the kind of person whose role he has been assigned.

5.   When this information has been gathered he should write a daily schedule for himself as a person in this role, telling what he or she does from the time he arises in the morning until the end of the working day,

or...

the student may describe such a typical day in the role of this person in paragraph form.

6. When students have described their "typical days", ask them to use their notes to share their "jobs" with the class.

7. Prepare a large poster or mural-size paper or use a section of the chalk board to make a permanent list entitled:

HOW MY GOVERNMENT WORKS TO KEEP ME SAFE AND HEALTHY

As students share their findings, add ideas to this list.

Note: Free material on different aspects of the Food and Drug Administration's scientific work is available from:

Bureau of Information & Education
Consumer Product Safety Commission
Washington, D. C.  20207

# TOUR THE STATES

Purpose:    After completing this activity the student should be able
            to relate a variety of important facts about the fifty
            United States.

1.    Use the pattern on the following page to create a game board
      for this activity.  (The pages may either be torn from this book
      and duplicated directly or an opaque projector may be used to
      trace an enlargement of the pattern.)

2.    Paste the "Go Card" pages on heavy tagboard and cut on the dotted
      lines.

3.    Use small blocks or other objects as "tour cars".

4.    Two to six players may play at one
      time.  At his turn each player
      draws a "go card".  He must follow
      the directions given on the card.
      The card will tell the player when
      and how many spaces to move.

5.    Declare the game over when one player has completed the tour.

6.    As students become familiar with the game and its facts, ask them
      to create new "go cards" to add to the game.

              Extension:

              Declare "State-of-the-Day" each day
              for a week or two weeks, choosing
              representative states from five general
              geographical areas.  Ask students to
              outline a plan of study and activity for
              application to each of the states studied.

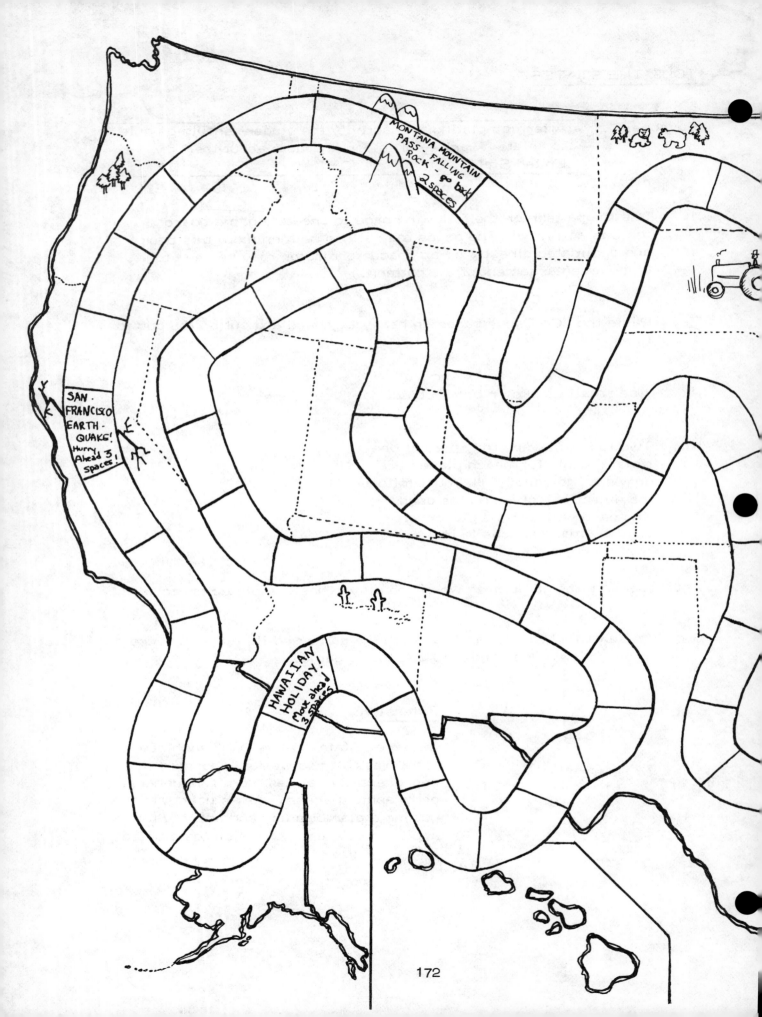

MONTANA MOUNTAIN PASS - FALLING ROCK - go back 2 spaces

SAN FRANCISCO EARTH- QUAKE! Hurry Ahead 3 Spaces!

HAWAIIAN HOLIDAY! Move ahead 3 spaces

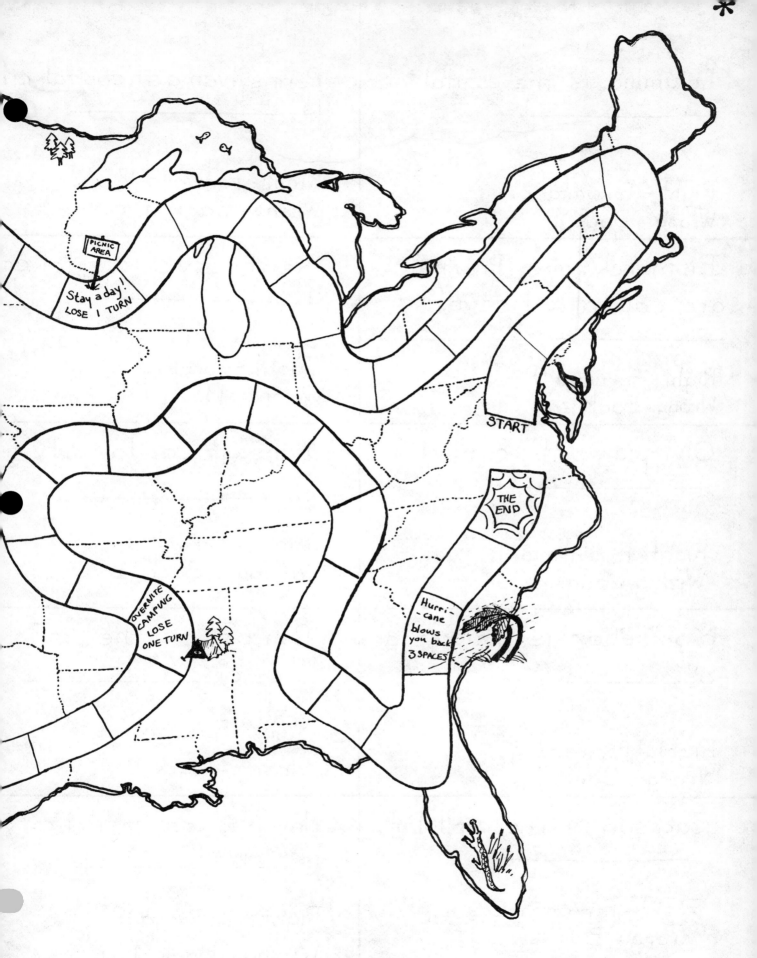

PICNIC
AREA
Stay a day!
LOSE 1 TURN

OVERNITE
CAMPING
LOSE
ONE TURN

START

THE
END

Hurri-
-cane
blows
you back
3 SPACES

Columbia is the capital of
_____ .

Right – Forward 2
Wrong – Back 1

---

Pennsylvania's capital cit
is _____ . ●

Right – Forward 2
Wrong – Back 1

---

Bismarck and Pierre
are capital cities of
_____ & _____

Right – Forward 4
Wrong – Back 2

---

Kentucky's capital cit
is _____ .

Right – Forward 2
Wrong – Back 1

---

Olympia is the capital of
_____ .

Right – Forward 3
Wrong – Back 1

---

Kansas' capital city
is _____ . ●

Right – Forward 2
Wrong – Back 1

---

Montpelier is the capital
of _____ .

Right – Forward 3
Wrong – Back 1

---

Concord is the capital
city of _____ .

Right – Forward 2
Wrong – Back 1

---

Jackson is the capital of
_____ .

Right – Forward 2
Wrong – Back 1

---

New Mexico's capital city
is _____ . ●

Right – Forward 2
Wrong – Back 1

174

The names of three states are spelled with only four letters each. Move one space for each one you can name.

Eight states have names that begin with the letter M. Move one space for each you can name.

Name the states where you'd find these people:
Hoosiers Tarheels Sooners
Move ahead one space for each.

In what state would you find the Grand Canyon?

One space.

In what state might you see a volcanic eruption?

One space.

In what state would you find Pike's Peak ?

One space.

In what state would you find Mt. McKinley ?

One space.

In what state would you find Niagara Falls ?

One space.

In what state would you find the Statue of Liberty?

One space.

In what state would you find the Liberty Bell ?

One space.

Name this state.

2 spaces

Name this state.

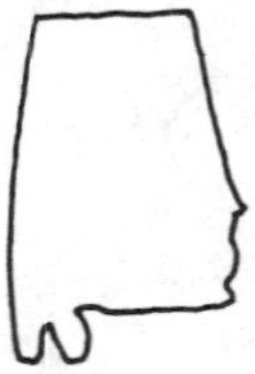

2 spaces

Name this state.

2 spaces

Name this state.

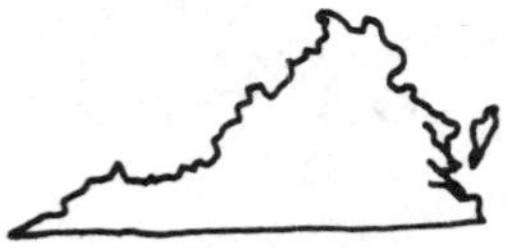

2 spaces

Name this state.

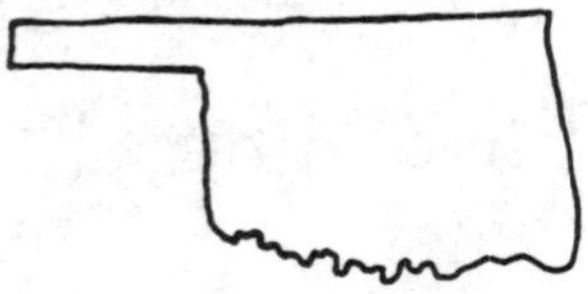

2 spaces

Name this state.

2 spaces

Name this state.

2 spaces

Name this state.

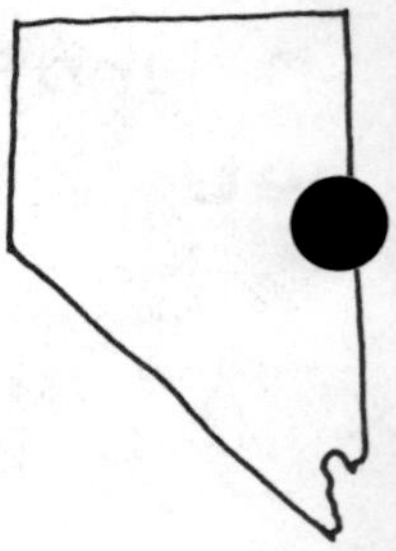

2 spaces

Name this state.

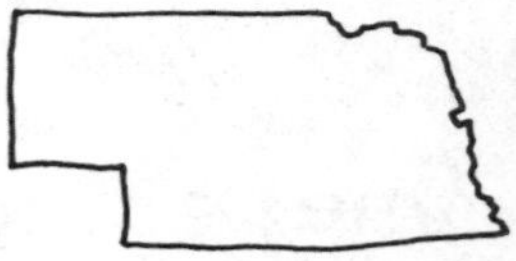

2 spaces

Name this state.

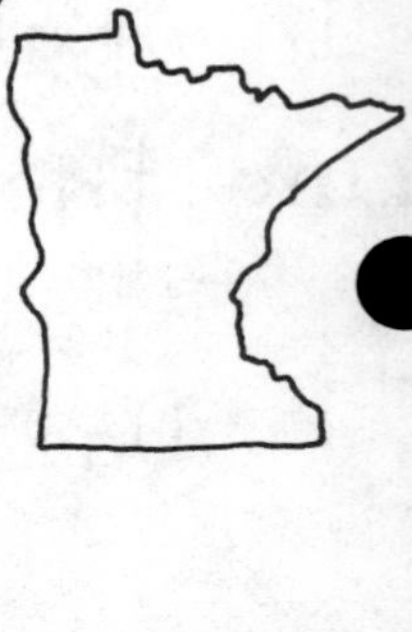

2 spaces

In what state would you find Mt. Rushmore?

One space.

What state is shaped like a mitten?

One space.

What state is completely surrounded by water?

One space.

Name three state capitals that may have been named after famous people.

One space for each.

Name three states that touch the Atlantic Ocean.

One space for each.

Name three states that touch Lake Michigan.

One space for each.

Name three states that touch the Pacific west coast.

One space for each.

Name three states that border the Gulf of Mexico.

One space for each.

Name three states that border the Mississippi River.

One space for each.

177

In what state would you find the Alamo?

One space.

# TRIP PLANNERS

**Purpose:** After completing this activity the student should be able to plan a trip to a designated site.

1.  Print the following list on the chalk board or a chart:

    A Major League Baseball Game
    A Scenic National Park
    A Seashore Resort
    A Skiing Vacation
    A Major Art Museum
    A Tour of a Movie Studio
    A Cool, Dry Climate
    A Desert Hideaway
    A Restored Plantation Home
    A Dude Ranch
    A Former President's Birthplace
    A Shopping Expedition
    A Mountain Retreat

2.  Provide encyclopedias, reference books (see Bibliography), airline, bus and train schedules, travel brochures, United States maps, pencils, and paper.

3.  Ask each student to select one topic from the list to use as the focal point of a trip he would like to take, and to use the reference materials to find the exact site he would visit.

4.  Distribute copies of the Planners' Guide on the following page and instruct each student to use the guide and appropriate reference materials in planning a trip to the selected site.

5.  After all the trips have been planned, arrange a time for sharing and discussing the plans in a group setting. Encourage students to present reference books, pictures, and maps in the sharing session.

## PLANNERS' GUIDE

1. Trip Focus (selected from the list) _____

2. Place to be visited _____
                            (city)                       (state)

3. Number of miles from home _____

4. Means of transportation to be used _____

   _____
   (Be sure to check to see if air, train, or bus service is available
   all or part of the way.  You may need to plan to use more than
   one means of transportation.)

5. Time necessary for journey:

       Planned departure time _____

       Planned arrival time _____

6. Will there be a time change?  If so, how much? _____

   _____

7. How much money will you need for the trip? _____

   What will the round trip transportation cost be? _____

8. How many days will you need to stay to accomplish the goals of
   the trip?
   _____

9. What kind of living accommodations will be available? ____

   _____

10. Approximately how much should you budget for housing and food?

   _____

11. What kind of clothes will you need to take? _____

   _____

# UNCLE SAM'S FAMILY

Purpose: After completing this activity the student should be able to demonstrate understanding of the meaning of United States citizenship.

1. Provide a variety of reference books, pamphlets, and leaflets related to the procedures and requirements for obtaining United States citizenship.

2. Lead a class discussion of the meaning of citizenship and the procedure necessary for acquiring United States citizenship.

3. Ask the students to pretend they have just arrived in this country and desire to become naturalized citizens. Direct them to work individually or in pairs to find out what information is required, the length of the waiting period, monetary cost, and what the privileges and demands will be.

4. Lead a class discussion to develop a definition of citizenship that is acceptable to all members of the group. Write the definition on the chalk board. Then read together the "Oath of Allegiance" taken by a naturalized citizen. (See World Book Encyclopedia, Volume C.)

5.    Use an oatmeal box or large potato chip can to create a replica of "Uncle Sam's" hat.

6.    Write the words and phrases below on numbered 3 x 5" cards.

jus soli                naturalization
citizen                 civic rights
non-citizen nationals    civic duty
jus sanguinis         political rights
dual nationality      14th Amendment
oath of allegiance    expatriation
stateless person

7.    Place the hat in a study center where resource materials are available. Ask students to visit the center in turn and choose eight or more cards from the hat.

8.    On his own paper the student should record the card number, copy the word or phrase, and write in his own words a definition of the term.

(A list of defined terms may be attached to the outside bottom of the hat for use as a self-checking device.)

## VISITOR'S EXCHANGE

Purpose:       After completing this activity the student should be able to compare and contrast family life styles.

1.     Use the mural completed in the "A Home is More Than a House" activity as motivation for a class discussion of how families living in each of the different types of homes represented are apt to live. Discuss urban and rural settings, affluent homes set on large acreages, small houses on busy streets, farm houses fronting on a major highway as well as pasture farm scenes, houseboats anchored along the shore, homes on an Indian reservation, big-city housing project homes, caretakers' cottages on large estates, duplexes, forest and lakeside cottages, mobile homes, and any others included in the mural.

2.     Guide the discussion to focus on likenesses and differences one would expect to find in family life styles on the basis of the homes they live in. Introduce topics such as:

                 (1) How the family income is derived
                 (2) Time the family gets up and goes to bed
                 (3) Means of transportation
                 (4) Recreation
                 (5) Clothes
                 (6) Kind of food
                 (7) Chores for adults and children

        Give emphasis to the concept of unique advantages to many life styles as opposed to the "best way".

3.     Ask each student to select the type of home in which he or she would most like to spend a week's vacation.

4.     Give the following instructions:

        Pretend you will be exchanging one-week visits with a boy or girl of your own age who lives in the home you have selected. Write a letter to the boy or girl telling them about your home and about the visit you have planned for them. He or she will want to know how to travel to your home, where and how you will meet him, the kind of clothes to bring, what you have planned for fun, and anything else special they should know about the vacation.

Recopy your letter carefully so that it is neatly
and legibly written and is as interesting as you
can make it.  Fold and address it by printing on
the outside:

Select a classmate with whom you can exchange
letters.  You receive your friend's letter to the
make-believe friend and answer it as if you were
the person to whom it was written.  Give the same
kind of information about the projected visit to the
make-believe friend's home as you did in the first
letter.  You may have to do some research in
reference books in order to effectively interpret
the life of your classmate's make-believe friend.

Exchange letters with your classmate and discuss
both letters.

WE, THE PEOPLE

Purpose: After completing this activity the student should be able to demonstrate his awareness of Americans as descendants from many other cultures and countries and identify some of the contributions made by these groups to our country.

1. Duplicate the following student pages for use as study and information guides.

2. Ask students to complete the map activity and the family interview as directed.

3. Provide a time when results of family interviews may be shared and findings may be interpreted and discussed.

Read the following paragraph and use the information there to show on the map where communities of people from other countries have settled in the United States.

You may write in the names of these groups on the map, or use a color key to code a color map.

Where did Americans come from? Except for Indians, Eskimos, and Hawaiians, almost everyone in the United States is a newcomer...or his parents, grandparents, or great-grandparents were. The early explorers were the first foreigners to bring settlers to America. Among them were the Dutch, Spanish, French, and English. Then the Pilgrims made their journeys. The English came to Jamestown and Plymouth. The Dutch came to New York and the Swedish to Delaware. Germans settled the state of Pennsylvania, and the French came to South Carolina and later, Louisiana. Negro slaves were brought to work on the southern plantations. Later, people went west. More Germans came to farm in Iowa and Pennsylvania. A Dutch settlement grew in what is now Michigan. Swedish and Norwegian farm families settled in Illinois, Wisconsin, Minnesota, Nebraska, and the Dakotas. Chinese and Japanese came to California and Spanish and Mexican settlers moved across the border into Texas, New Mexico, and California. Later Puerto Ricans and Cubans began to come to Florida and many of them went on north to Chicago, New York, and the other large American cities. We are a people made up of many other peoples. We have brought with us the customs and traditions and beliefs of many lands. Some of these we have cherished and saved. Others we have given up to make a new way for a new kind of community in a new environment. This is America.

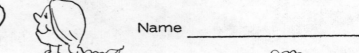

Name _____

## WHERE DID WE COME FROM?

Choose three families in your neighborhood and interview them. Then interview your own parents or grandparents to find the information for this questionnaire:

| | Family I | Family II | Family III | Your Family |
|---|---|---|---|---|
| **What is the family name?** | | | | |
| **From what other countries did they or their ancestors come?** | | | | |
| **Why did they come to America?** | | | | |
| **What special customs and traditions from the other countries do they still observe?** | | | | |

YOUR LAND IS MY LAND

Purpose: After completing this activity the student should be able to identify several national parks and relate the intent and purpose of maintaining these areas of natural resource.

1.   Prior to this activity ask a very able student to look up National Parks or National Park Service in an encyclopedia or resource book and prepare a brief presentation for the class explaining the purpose and origin of national parks and monuments.

Ask that this presentation emphasize the national parks as preservations of American heritage--America's vast wilderness, scenery, and history, as well as its splendid vacationlands.

2.   After this brief presentation and appropriate discussion, present the following list of addresses:

National Park Service Regional Offices

The National Park Service is a bureau of the Department of the Interior, with headquarters in Washington, D. C. There are six regional offices:

(1) Southeast Regional Office, Federal Building, Box 10008, 400 North Eighth Street, Richmond, Virginia 23240, has jurisdiction over areas in Alabama, Arkansas, Florida, Georgia, Kentucky, Louisiana, Mississippi, North and South Carolina, Tennessee, Virginia, Puerto Rico, and the Virgin Islands.

(2) Midwest Regional Office, 1709 Jackson Street, Omaha, Nebraska 68102, has jurisdiction over areas in Iowa, Kansas, Minnesota, Missouri, Montana, Nebraska, North and South Dakota, Wyoming, and Colorado (except Mesa Verde National Park).

(3) Southwest Regional Office, Old Santa Fe Trail, P. O. Box 728, Santa Fe, New Mexico 87501, has jurisdiction over areas in Arizona, New Mexico, Oklahoma, Texas, Utah, and Mesa Verde National Park in Colorado.

(4) Western Regional Office, 450 Golden Gate Avenue, P. O. Box 36063, San Francisco, California 94102, has jurisdiction over areas in California, Idaho, Nevada, Oregon, Washington, Alaska, and Hawaii.

(5) Northeast Regional Office, 143 South Third Street, Philadelphia, Pennsylvania 19106, has jurisdiction over areas in Connecticut, Delaware, Illinois, Indiana, Maine, Maryland, Massachusetts, Michigan, New Hampshire, New Jersey, New York, Ohio, Pennsylvania, Rhode Island, Vermont, and Wisconsin.

(6) National Capital Regional Office, 1100 Ohio Drive, S. W., Washington, D. C. 20242, has jurisdiction over areas in and around the national capital.

3.  Ask each student or small groups of students to prepare a letter to one of the regional offices of the National Park Service requesting information, brochures, etc. related to the parks in that area.

4.  Ask students to use this information and other resource materials in the classroom or school library to prepare a visually exciting poster or mural-size piece of promotional advertising about one or more of the parks in that region. These pieces should be designed to entice travelers to visit the chosen national park and provide them with pertinent information about what kinds of things they might expect to see and do there.

5.  Provide a special time for students to present their projects and a large space such as a hallway or cafeteria wall where they may exhibit the finished posters and murals where other students may learn from and enjoy them.

188

# THE WORLD AND BEYOND

notes . . . .

# AROUND THE WORLD IN SEVEN DAYS

Purpose: After completing this activity the student should be able to discuss knowledgeably and appreciatively the seven continents of the world.

1. Provide a good collection of resource materials for studying the seven continents. The collection should include reference books, maps, a globe, pictures, film strips, magazines, pamphlets, and social studies texts (see Bibliography).

2. Set the stage for an armchair trip around the world by inviting the students to join you in preparing an entry for an imaginary contest to select the class most suited for world travel. Tell them that:

   (1) All entries must be composite class efforts; no applications will be accepted from individual students.

   (2) All entries must cover the entire world, with specific attention given to each of the seven continents.

   (3) Entering classes must submit a full application packet, including reasons for wanting to visit each of the seven continents, some information about the continent, how the time there will be spent, and a plan for using and sharing the knowledge gained from the trip.

3. Divide the class into seven work groups and instruct the students to use resource materials to prepare contest entry packets for each of the seven continents. Suggest the use of a variety of art materials to make the final efforts colorful and attractive.

4. Allow sufficient time for study and final packet preparation before collecting and compiling the packets to constitute the final contest entry.

5. Set aside seven consecutive days for the groups to present collected data to the class. Encourage each group to plan a creative presentation such as a panel discussion, creative drama or role playing, costumes and props, use of graphic or audio aids, foods, crafts, and other media.

6. Add the compiled packets to the classroom social studies materials collection for future reference.

Adaptation and Extension:

A mural reflecting the planned trip would add interest to the project.

The same plan could be adapted to a study of one nation or one state.

# CONTINENTAL TRIOS

Purpose: After completing this activity the student should be able to express factual knowledge of the seven continents.

1. Write on three squares of tagboard facts about each of the seven continents (three cards for Africa, three for Asia, three for Antarctica, three for Europe, three for Australia, etc.)

2. Draw pictures of the continents on seven squares.

3. Laminate the squares or cover them with plastic wrap.

4. Cover a small stationery box with an old world map (or ask a group of students to reproduce and color the world map in the appendix of this book) to make a container for the game cards. Label the box "Continental Trios".

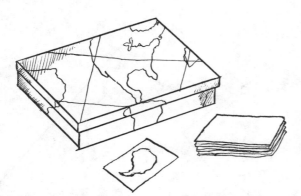

5. Prepare a game direction card with the following instructions.

## Continental Trios

(1)  This game is for three players.

(2)  Shuffle and deal the cards, seven cards to each player, with one in the center of the table.

(3)  Look at your cards to find trios. (Three fact cards about one continent will make a trio.) Place all trios on the table.

(4)  Begin to draw cards by drawing from the player to the left. Each player may elect to draw from the player to the left or to exchange one card in his hand for the card on the table. Place trios on the table as cards are drawn to complete one.

(5)  If a continent picture card is drawn it may be added to the trio stack only when the player holding it has already placed the trio on the table.

6. The round continues until one player is out of cards and wins the round.

7. Keep score at the end of each round with the winner receiving seven points, and other players receiving one point for each trio topped by a continent picture card. Completed trios without a continent picture card receive no points.

8. Continue the game for seven rounds. The player with the highest score at the end of the seventh round wins the game.

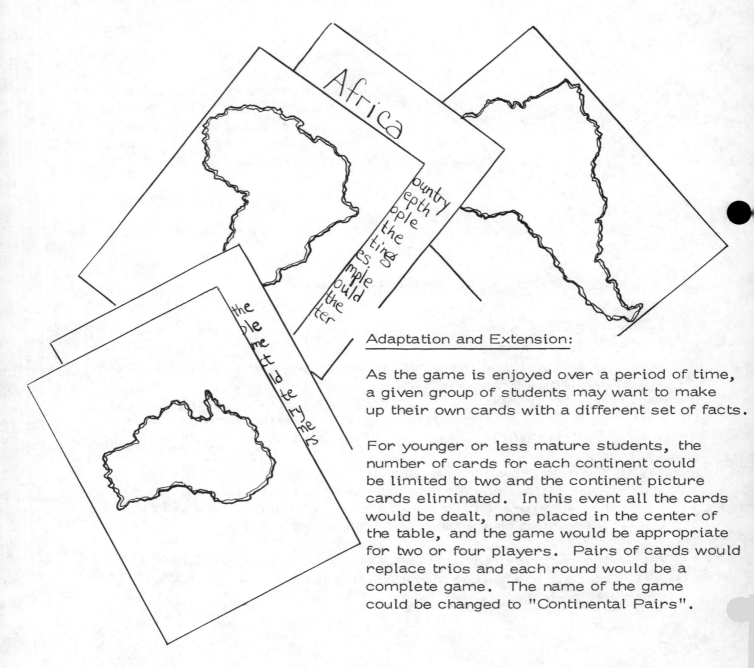

Adaptation and Extension:

As the game is enjoyed over a period of time, a given group of students may want to make up their own cards with a different set of facts.

For younger or less mature students, the number of cards for each continent could be limited to two and the continent picture cards eliminated. In this event all the cards would be dealt, none placed in the center of the table, and the game would be appropriate for two or four players. Pairs of cards would replace trios and each round would be a complete game. The name of the game could be changed to "Continental Pairs".

## COOK'S TOUR

Purpose: After completing this activity the student should be able to demonstrate increased awareness of food as representative of the cultural heritage, customs, and traditions related to a given people.

1. Discuss food as derivative of cultural pride, tradition, and preference.

2. Ask each student to choose a nation or country whose culinary traditions and tastes he would like to explore.

3. Prepare a brief letter to parents explaining plans for a culinary tour of nations and asking each to assist his child in supplying one recipe for a favorite foreign dish.

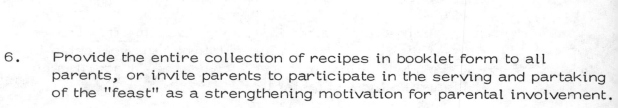

4. Choose several recipes from these that will be used in the preparation of an "international feast".

5. Prepare the dishes at school with ingredients for each being provided by parents, or students may prepare the dishes at home, assisted by their parents, and bring them to school at a designated time.

6. Provide the entire collection of recipes in booklet form to all parents, or invite parents to participate in the serving and partaking of the "feast" as a strengthening motivation for parental involvement.

7. Have each student dress in the traditional festive clothing of the country from which his recipe originates on the "feast day" (if possible) and have him serve that dish to the group.

# FAR-OUT FRONTIER

Purpose: After completing this activity the student should be able to identify and organize information pertinent to a given topic.

1. Create a learning center which resembles the interior of a space capsule. Provide a "space helmet", "control panel", etc., including a tape recorder with pre-recorded tape containing information on space travel. The message for the taping follows.

"A message to all space men and women--welcome aboard Command Module for Moonbeam IV.

"The command module is like a small room in which the astronauts will live while they are in space. In this room they control the rocket engines and all the equipment they need to make the rocket go to the moon and bring them back to earth.

"Soon we will be ready for the countdown. The countdown begins counting hours, then minutes. Finally, it will count seconds: 10, 9, 8, 7, 6, 5, 4, 3, 2, 1, fire. If anything goes wrong, the countdown will be interrupted until everything is fixed and working properly.

"At the end of the countdown you will hear the command for ignition. Ignition means to catch fire. This happens when the rocket fuel and oxygen mix and an electric spark starts them burning. Then fiery gases shoot out of the bottom of the space rocket and it slowly begins to move upward from the ground.

"Immediately after ignition comes lift-off. This is the beginning of the flight into space. It is when the spaceship lifts off the ground. First it moves slowly, then it goes faster and faster and faster and faster!

"Hey, do you know anything about where you're going? Where is space? What is it? Did you know that space has nothing in it--not even air? There is no air in outer space or on the moon. When an astronaut gets out of the spaceship, he must wear a special space suit which carries a supply of oxygen. Without it he could not breathe or live.

"After a trip into space, the astronauts must return to earth. This coming back into the atmosphere surrounding the earth can be pretty tricky. There is danger of the spaceship becoming very hot and burning up. This coming back to earth is called re-entry.

"A metal cover on the bottom side of the spaceship will protect the astronauts during re-entry. This cover is called a heatshield.

"As the spaceship returns to earth, gravity causes it to move very fast through the atmosphere, and it becomes very hot. This heatshield protects the spaceship from most of the heat and keeps it from burning up.

"After a safe re-entry comes a nice, cool splashdown. Splashdown is the spaceship's landing at sea. It is much easier and softer to land on water than on land.

"After splashdown, swimmers called "frogmen" and helicopters will help to get the spacemen out of the spaceship and back to a ship which can carry them safely to land again.

"What an exciting experience a space trip must be! If you were an astronaut on such a trip you would have to keep many notes and records on your trip. These records are called "flight logs". The information astronauts keep on their logs is very important for helping men to learn about space.

"Read your 'space log' carefully, and see what information is needed to complete it. Then listen to the tape again to find the information you need to fill in your log. Complete the log carefully.

"Be a super-good astronaut!"

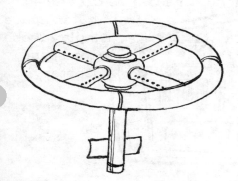

2.    Place duplicated copies of the "space log" in the center.

3.    Ask students who visit the center to listen carefully to the
      pre-recorded tape, sort out the information needed to complete
      the "space log", and fill in facts and answers to questions with
      appropriate responses.

4.    After each student has completed the "space log", ask him to
      choose one of the following topics or projects for further exploration
      of space travel:

      (1)    Using all available information and a lot of imagination,
             describe the first moon base.  What will it look like?
             How will people live there?  How will they get supplies?

      (2)    Make a list of United States astronauts, their names, and
             location of their homes.  Write a short one-paragraph
             history of each man's life before he became an astronaut.

      (3)    Make a model or diagram of one of the United States
             spaceships or design a future spaceship of your own.

      (4)    Make a space "glossary" of words and terms associated
             with space travel.  Illustrate as many words as possible.

      (5)    Read at least three short books on space travel and design
             an attractive advertisement for each on a 5 x 7" index card.
             Place them in the space center where other students will
             see them and may be attracted to the same books.

      (6)    Create your own project on one of the following topics:

             a.    The United States "moon bug"
             b.    Phases of the moon
             c.    Lunar docking and moon exploration
             d.    Rocks from the moon
             e.    Mission Control
             f.    Space suits

      (7)    Make one or more "space masks" which characterize creatures
             from outer space.
             Display these in
             the space
             center.

5.  Provide a varied selection of resource books, pictures, articles, and related materials for reference (see Bibliography).

6.  Ask students to prepare a brief written report, including at least one illustration, to add to a notebook on Space Exploration which will be kept in the classroom or school library.

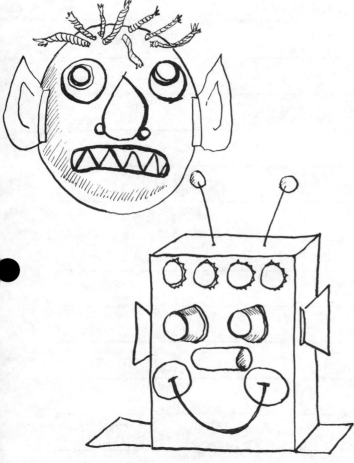

Adaptation:

To make the space center more interesting, several facts, figures, and illustrated items of information related to space may be introduced as part of the control panel, flight maps, logs, etc. The tape-recorded message may direct students to each source of information.

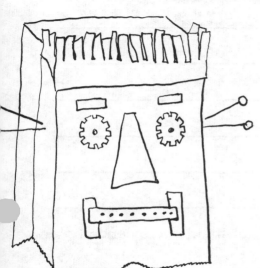

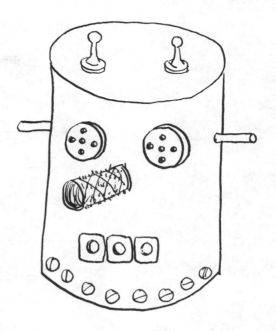

FAR–OUT FRONTIER – SPACE LOG

Time of Entry _____

Astronaut _____

| Terms | Description of Terms |
|---|---|

command module _____

_____

*ignition _____

_____

heatshield _____

_____

frogmen _____

_____

*re–entry _____

_____

space _____

_____

*countdown _____

_____

*lift–off _____

_____

*splashdown _____

_____

List the terms which are starred above in order of their occurrence on a space flight.

_____

# FIESTA FANFARE

Purpose:    After completing this activity the student should be able
            to express understanding and appreciation for some
            aspects of Mexican culture.

1.    Assemble a good collection of resource books, pictures, maps,
      and other media dealing with significant aspects of geography,
      history, and cultural mores associated with Mexico.

2.    Point to Mexico on a world map and explain within the framework
      of class discussion that this country is especially important to
      us because it is a neighboring country and that Mexico and the
      United States depend on many cultural and economic exchanges.

3.    Introduce Mexico as a beautiful country full of
      contrasts.  Lead the discussion to focus on
      physical features ranging from mountains to
      deserts and beaches, on the wide range between
      rustic rural villages to Mexico City which is
      one of the most sophisticated cities in the world,
      the many different backgrounds, goals, and life
      styles of the people, the influence of tourism
      and industrialization on life today, and many
      other fascinating aspects of life in Mexico.

4.    Culminate the session with discussion of a
      Mexican fiesta as representative of the love
      for color, pageantry, ceremony, and merry-
      making that has traditionally been important
      to the Mexican people.  Write the word fiesta
      on the chalk board.  Discuss the tradition of
      village fiestas to honor local patron saints
      and of the evolution of music, food, flowers,
      dancing, and other aesthetic and social
      aspects of these celebrations as they have
      continued for many years.

5.    Ask the class to join you in planning a class Fiesta Day in honor of our
      neighbors "south of the border".  In preparation for the fiesta ask the
      class to divide into small groups to research one of the following topics
      and assume responsibility for a contribution to the fiesta celebration
      that will represent that phase of Mexican culture.

|            |        |         |
|------------|--------|---------|
| Costumes   | Food   | Music   |
| Decorations| Crafts | Dancing |
| Parade     | Games  | History |

201

6.  Set aside a day for the fiesta and plan to devote the entire school
    day (if possible) to the celebration.  Enlist support of the cafeteria
    staff, music, or other special teachers insofar as possible to add
    extra "zing" to the day.  Encourage small groups to use ingenuity in
    carrying out their responsibilities.

    Have fun!  There's no better way to make a project meaningful
    and memorable!

### Extension and Adaptation:

This activity might be modified for
less mature students by using a film
strip for the introduction and limiting
the fiesta activities to those that can
be planned and presented with a
minimum of "outside" preparation.

Lots of multicolor crepe paper for
bunting, paper flowers, and streamers,
recorded music, a pinata, serapes, and
Mexican pottery will add background
color and excitement to the day.

If school rules and the budget (for
food and favors) permit, it would be
nice to invite another class to be
fiesta guests for all or part of the day.

# FOOD FARE

Purpose:      After completing this activity the student should be able to demonstrate increased understanding of the origin and production of common foods.

1.     Secure a copy of a menu soon to be served in the school cafeteria.

2.     Present the menu to the class and ask the students to work in small groups to determine the origin, production, processing steps, transportation, and preparation necessary for each item to reach the luncheon table.

3.     Arrange time and resources to facilitate use of texts, encyclopedias, library materials, and interviews with the dietician, cook, or principal.

4.     Encourage the small groups to be creatively thorough in preparing oral reports to be presented to the total group.

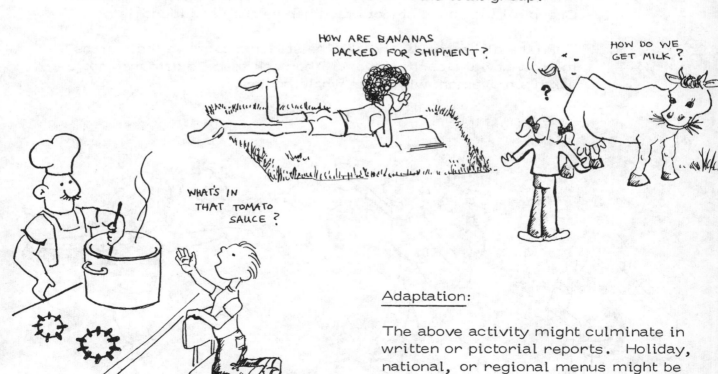

Adaptation:

The above activity might culminate in written or pictorial reports. Holiday, national, or regional menus might be used.

GLOBE SPOTTERS

Purpose:     After completing this activity the student should be able
             to develop awareness of the shape and motion of the
             earth.

1.   Provide a globe, flat world map, orange, round balloon, rubber ball,
     round wooden bead, pencil, drinking straw, paper cone, square
     block, and other objects of various shapes.

2.   Place all of the objects on
     a table or designated space
     on the floor.  Ask the students
     to sit in a semi-circle around
     the objects.

3.   Present the globe and print the word globe on the chalk board.
     Compare the globe and flat map, and explain that the globe is a
     round map of the world.  Discuss the concept of the globe as a
     symbol of the world, emphasizing the fact that the real world is
     much larger.

4.   Tell the students that the globe is round because it represents
     the world which is round.  Ask one student at a time to select
     one object from the display that is the same shape as the earth.
     Group all the round objects together as they are identified.

5.   Turn the globe slowly and ask the students to move their arms
     to show how the earth moves.  Then ask them to demonstrate the
     earth's movement with their whole bodies.

6.  Write the word axis on the board and demonstrate with the globe
    the concept that the world turns on its axis. Clarify the concept
    by using a styrofoam ball and a drinking straw to demonstrate
    the motion of the earth.

Adaptation:

More mature students may profit
from locating their own continent,
country, and state on the globe.

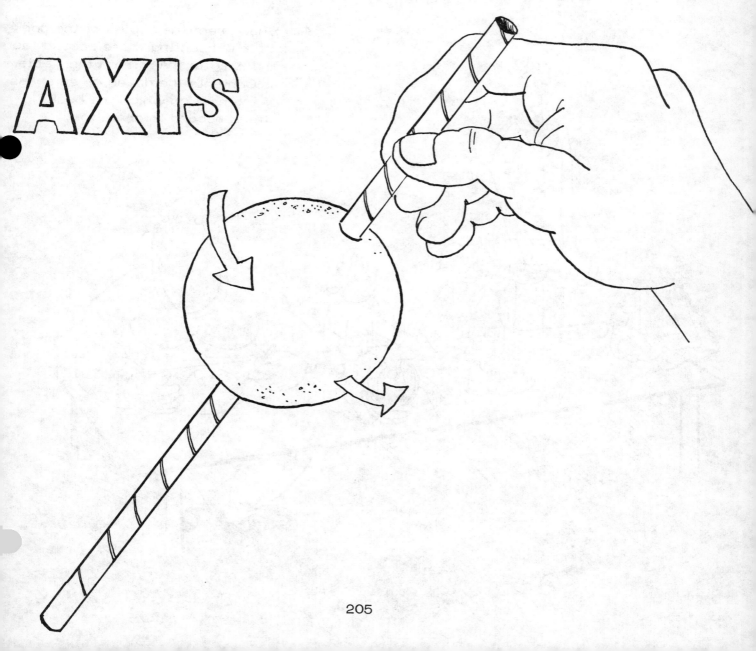

AXIS

# GUINESS GOURMET BUFFET

Purpose:    After completing this activity the student should be able
to demonstrate awareness of the importance of record-
breaking in our human society and should exhibit renewed
interest in a variety of world affairs, as well as having
become acquainted with the Guiness Book of World Records.

1.    Obtain several copies of the latest Guiness Book of World Records.

2.    Choose at least ten items of interest from this book to share with
your students as motivation for reading the book themselves.

3.    Present these in a How Would You Like to Know session--choose
items that will surprise and excite them.

4.    Show them the copies of the book
after presenting these record facts.
and read to them from the Table
of Contents the dozen or so areas
of interest on which the book
offers record information.

5.	Divide students into small groups and ask each group to be responsible for one area:

> The Human Being
> The Animal & Plant Kingdoms
> The Natural World
> The Universe & Space
> The Scientific World
> The Arts & Entertainment
> The Business World
> The World's Structures
> The Mechanical World
> The Human World
> Human Achievements
> Sports, Games & Pastimes

6.	Ask each group to read carefully their section of the <u>Guiness Book of World Records</u> and choose six to eight facts they feel will be of general interest to the class.

7.	Have the groups then think of some unusual or creative way to present these facts to the class.  They may use pantomime, , pictures, movies, drama, art, shadow plays, overhead projector, body painting, puppet shows, radio or television shows, a newspaper format, giant book, table mats, miniature museum display, outdoor tour, etc.

8.	Set aside one afternoon or special session for a "Guiness Gourmet Buffet" or some such exciting event for sharing these record presentations.

HOW = IS EQUAL?

Purpose: After completing this activity the student should be able to demonstrate awareness of women's roles in today's society as perceived by members of the immediate community.

1. Reproduce and distribute copies of the questionnaire on the following page.

2. Ask each student to use the questionnaire as the focus of interviews with three people with different sex, age, and occupational backgrounds.

3. Elect within a group setting a student committee to tabulate and record the interview data, and a second committee to review the data and write implications.

4. Arrange for a panel discussion on the implications of the questionnaire data as a culminating activity. Invite an adult male and an adult female (mother, father, principal, teacher, etc.) to serve on the panel, and conduct a student election to select one boy, one girl, and a moderator from the class. Encourage follow-up discussion by the total group.

Interviewer's Name _____

Date _____

DATA ON PERSON INTERVIEWED

Name _____

Age _____ Sex _____ Occupation _____

1.  Do you think women and men today have equal civil rights?

    _____

2.  Do you think women can do most jobs as well as men?

    _____

3.  What are some jobs (if any) you think only men should have?

    _____

4.  What are some jobs (if any) you think only women should have?

    _____

5.  When men and women hold the same jobs do you think they should
    be paid the exact same salaries? _____

6.  In households where both the husband and wife are employed outside
    the home, do you think the household chores should be shared 50–50?

    _____

7.  If not, how should they be shared? _____

8.  Do you think women should be encouraged to run for political office?

    _____

9.  Would you vote for a woman for President of the United States?

    _____

# IM-MATCH-INATION MAP

| Purpose: | After completing this activity the student should be able to locate strategic areas in world geography and give limited facts related to each area. |
|---|---|

1.  Use the world outline map available in the appendix. Duplicate enough copies for all students.

2.  Duplicate the following pages of "Matchables" so that each student may have one full set.

3.  Direct students to paste the world map in the center of a piece of construction paper at least 18 x 24" in size. (Pages from a large wallpaper book are a good substitute, or one-half sheets of newspaper may be used.)

4.  Instruct the students to cut the "matchables" from their pages and paste them on or as near to their appropriate geographical location as possible. (When space is not available he may paste the pictures around the edge of the map and draw arrows from them to their appropriate areas.) Students may color maps and "matchables" if they so desire.

5.  Ask the student to justify each "match" he has made in his completed project.

## STATED STRANGELY

**Purpose:** After completing this activity the student should be able to identify names of states of the United States.

1.  Duplicate the following page to provide one for each pupil.

2.  Ask students to read each sentence carefully to find the name of a state hidden in each. (They should circle or underline each answer.)

3.  Ask students to use the list of states and capitals at the bottom of the page to create additional riddles.

4.  Have each student create at least five to ten riddles to add to a large class game which identifies many states and capitals.

| States: | Capitals: | States: | Capitals: |
|---------|-----------|---------|-----------|
| Alabama | Montgomery | Montana | Helena |
| Alaska | Juneau | Nebraska | Lincoln |
| Arizona | Phoenix | Nevada | Carson City |
| Arkansas | Little Rock | New Hampshire | Concord |
| California | Sacramento | New Jersey | Trenton |
| Colorado | Denver | New Mexico | Santa Fe |
| Connecticut | Hartford | New York | Albany |
| Delaware | Dover | North Carolina | Raleigh |
| Florida | Tallahassee | North Dakota | Bismarck |
| Georgia | Atlanta | Ohio | Columbus |
| Hawaii | Honolulu | Oklahoma | Oklahoma City |
| Idaho | Boise | Oregon | Salem |
| Illinois | Springfield | Pennsylvania | Harrisburg |
| Indiana | Indianapolis | Rhode Island | Providence |
| Iowa | Des Moines | South Carolina | Columbia |
| Kansas | Topeka | South Dakota | Pierre |
| Kentucky | Frankfort | Tennessee | Nashville |
| Louisiana | Baton Rouge | Texas | Austin |
| Maine | Augusta | Utah | Salt Lake City |
| Maryland | Annapolis | Vermont | Montpelier |
| Massachusetts | Boston | Virginia | Richmond |
| Michigan | Lansing | Washington | Olympia |
| Minnesota | St. Paul | West Virginia | Charleston |
| Mississippi | Jackson | Wisconsin | Madison |
| Missouri | Jefferson City | Wyoming | Cheyenne |

There is a state in this common tan and brown house. Can you find it?

STATED STRANGELY

Name: _____

Find the hidden name of a state in each sentence.  Underline it.

1.  Jim and Ida hoed six rows of beans.

2.  Sally just got a darling new York terrier from her Uncle Bill.

3.   Color a dog brown and white.

4.  I hid the box in Diana's closet.

5.  Is he admired for his courage or giant strength?

6.  Ann Eva Dayton is a beautiful girl!

7.  If she should awaken, tuck your baby back in bed.

8.  Carla has a new jersey knit gown.

9.  You will miss our ideas when we are gone!

10.  The cabin was common tan and brown in color.

11.  We cheered Big Tex as he rode the wild horse.

12.  Codes of man made law are to live by.

13.  As we traveled south, Carol inadvertently followed the wrong signs.

14.  Mary landed her kite on the village green.

15.  Is the gold ore gone from Willow Cave?

16.  Take a picture of Lori dancing.

17.  Cherrio!  Hi!  Open the gate!  We're here!

18.  When I was ill, I noisily coughed and cleared my throat.

19.  When you go to the hospital, ask a doctor for help.

20.  Pay your bills weekly--never monthly.

BEWARE MAN-EATING TIGERS!

CAUTION: GIRAFFE CROSSING

EIFFEL TOWER

HIGHEST MOUNTAIN IN THE WORLD!

LEANING TOWER OF PISA

VOLKSWAGEN

VIKING SHIP

ARAB

WIND MILL

STATUE OF LIBERTY

TOMB OF THE UNKNOWN SOLDIER

END
OF THE
LONGEST
HIGHWAY
IN THE
WORLD

26,800
miles to go!

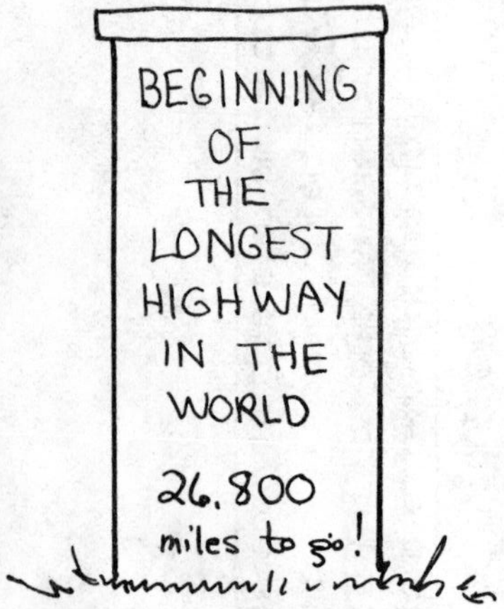

BEGINNING
OF
THE
LONGEST
HIGHWAY
IN THE
WORLD

LARGEST ANIMAL
SHELTER IN THE
WORLD!
Shoot elephants, lion,
zebra, rhino + birds
with your camera

IT'S NOT JUST TALK!

| Purpose: | After completing this activity the student should be able to identify the major means of communication, both historic and current, and be familiar with the people and events which contributed to their development. |

1.  Use the following pages to duplicate and prepare for each student a Glossary of Communications.

2.  Explain to the students the purpose of this activity as stated above, and encourage each to work on his own to research and discover the meanings and implications of terms included in the glossary.

3.  Assist less able students in completing the activity by forming small teacher-directed groups where help is given in locating information and using reference materials.

4.  Give each student a copy of the Communications Contract and provide a variety of resource books and materials, as well as library time, for them to complete their contract activities.

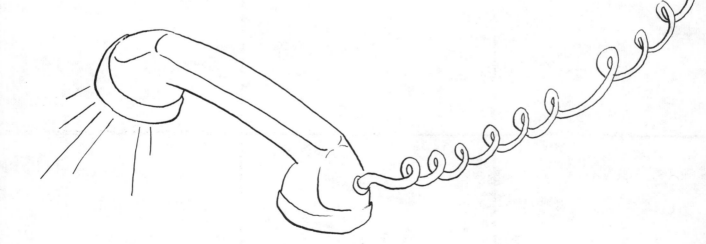

# Glossary of Communications

Advertising _____

_____

Alphabet _____

_____

_____

Bell, Alexander Graham _____

_____

_____

Braille System _____

_____

_____

Broadcasting _____

_____

_____

Codes _____

_____

Dictionary _____

_____

Edison, Thomas Alva _____

_____

hieroglyphics _____

_____

_____

Homing Pigeons _____

_____

_____

Indian Sign language _____

_____

Magnetic tape _____

_____

Marconi, Guglielmo _____

_____

Morse Code _____

_____

_____

Morse, Samuel F. B. _____

_____

Papyrus _____

_____

Parchment _____

_____

Phonetics _____

_____

Phonograph _____

_____

Photography _____

_____

_____

Pictographs _____

_____

_____

Printing Press _____

_____

Radar _____

_____

Sign language for the Deaf _____

_____

_____

Signals _____

_____

_____

Talbot, William Henry Fox. _____

_____

Telegraph _____

_____

Telephone _____

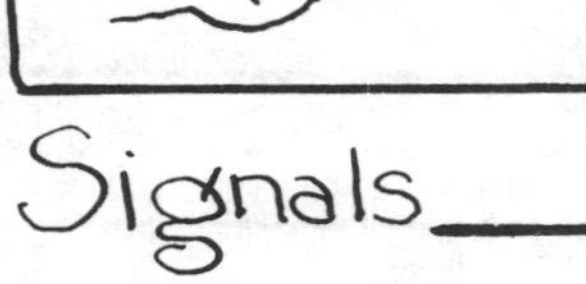

_____

_____

"What Hath God Wrought" _____

_____

# COMMUNICATIONS CONTRACT

Name _____

Choose one of the following projects related to the study of communications:

(1)    Draw a time-line showing the history and development of communications.

(2)    A stamp collection showing stamps related to communications

(3)    Read a biography and write a short report on the life of a person who made a vital contribution to the development of communications

(4)    Make a "scroll" movie about communication in ancient days

(5)    Write a short paragraph in Braille or learn several sentences in deaf sign language

(6)    Make a booklet of pictographs used in international travel.

(7)    On a tape recorder tell the story of the invention of the telephone, telegraph; phonograph, or motion pictures

(8)    Create your own project.  Describe your idea below and submit it to your teacher for approval.

_____

_____

_____

_____

_____

(Circle the project you have chosen to do.)

What is the first thing you will do to start your project? _____

_____

What sources will you use for information? _____

_____

_____

_____

What materials will you need to work with? _____

_____

_____

_____

How long do you expect your project to take? _____

_____

_____

_____

What kind of help or assistance will you need? _____

_____

_____

How do you expect to share your project with others? _____

_____

_____

_____

I will do my very best to complete the project I have chosen
as outlined above.

Signed _____

# LISTEN TO THE POET

Purpose:
> After completing this activity the student should be able
> to select and relate to poetry as a timely and creative
> reaction to the social structure of its time.

1. Provide a good collection of anthologies and other sources of poetry
   (see Bibliography), a sturdy loose-leaf notebook, unlined paper for
   the notebook, felt tip pens, and art materials.

2. Read two or three poems with socially reactive themes aloud
   and encourage student involvement in a discussion of the time,
   circumstances, and the poet's message in each poem.

   Suggested poems are:

   > "It's Almost the Year Two Thousand" – Robert Frost
   > "Prayers of Steel" – Carl Sandburg
   > "When Serpents Bargain for the Right to Squirm" –
   >    E. E. Cummings
   > "An Agony.  As Now." – LeRoi Jones

3. Culminate the discussion with an analysis of the value of poetry as
   social commentary on its own time.

4. Present the notebook and
   plans for compiling an
   anthology to be contributed
   to the school library.

5. Ask each student to:

   (1) Select one poem that deals with
       a period, event, goal, or life
       style reflective of one particular social phenomenon.

   (2) Copy the poem carefully on paper for the anthology.  Give
       credit to the author and source of the poem.

   (3) Select art materials to illustrate the poem.

   (4) Write a two- or three-paragraph critique of the poem
       interpreting the poet's viewpoint and possible message of
       the poem.

   (5) Add the illustrated poem and critique to the anthology.

6. Prepare a table of contents and index for the anthology.

7. Provide time for sharing the anthology in a group setting before presenting it to the school library.

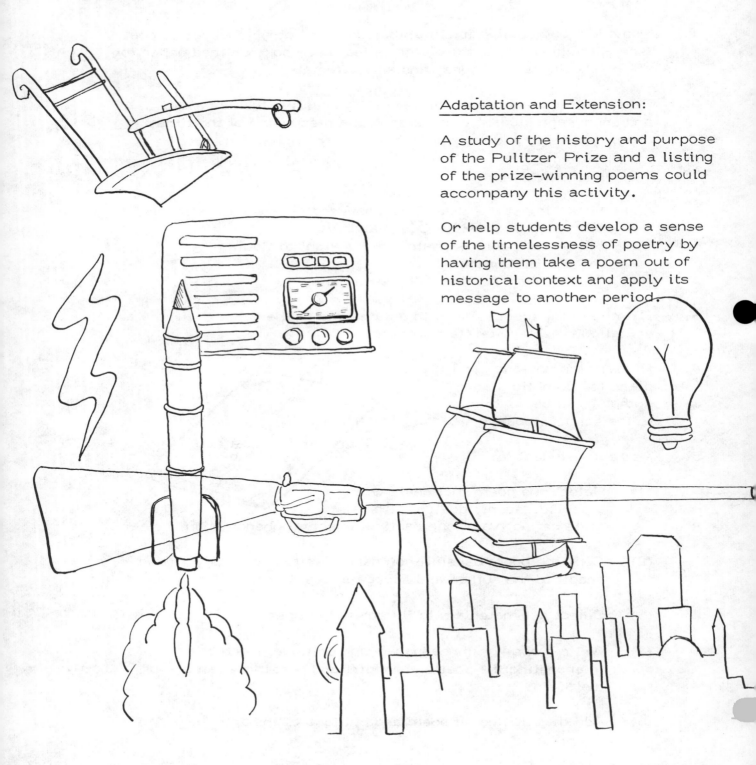

Adaptation and Extension:

A study of the history and purpose of the Pulitzer Prize and a listing of the prize-winning poems could accompany this activity.

Or help students develop a sense of the timelessness of poetry by having them take a poem out of historical context and apply its message to another period.

# MARKET PLACE, INTERNATIONAL

Purpose: After completing this activity the student should be able to creatively express understanding of the importance of world trade in daily life.

1. Ask students to contribute to a collection of items from countries other than the United States to be used to stock the market place. Stipulate that items must bear a label attesting to the place of origin.

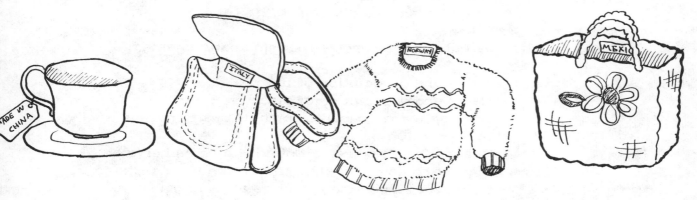

2. Arrange the items in an attractive display. Ask each student to select one item from the collection (without looking at the "made in _____" label) to use as a focal point for research on international trade.

3. Direct a class discussion of the influence of import and export practices on the present-day economic system. Encourage students to participate fully in the discussion by contributing ideas about the origin of objects from other countries that are ordinarily taken for granted, above relative costs of products produced in our own country and those imported from other countries, about the chief products manufactured in our country and sold to others, etc.

4. Culminate the discussion by giving the following directions:

    (1) Try to find out as much as you can about the circumstances under which your item is made and marketed. Some items may be labeled with the name of a city, a region, or a province, while others carry only the name of the country.

(2)    Use resource books, magazines (such as <u>National Geographic</u>), social studies books, and other sources to gather information about the following:

    a.    Place of origin
    b.    Raw materials used
    c.    Process involved in production of the item
    d.    Lives of the people
    e.    Economic concerns
    f.    Sales promotion
    g.    Shipping and handling

(3)    Use this outline to organize the information gained:

    a.    Name and description of item
    b.    Name and description of place of origin
    c.    Description of manufacturing or craft process involved in production
    d.    Reason for shipping to United States rather than marketing domestically; reason for United States to import rather than produce at home
    e.    Possible route "traveled" by item before reaching purchaser; packaging, shipping, and handling requirements
    f.    Number of people (identified by roles) involved in production of item and its distribution
    g.    Contribution of item to purchaser's life style; effects of doing without item and/or possible substitutions
    h.    Other facts of interest

(4)    Present your findings to the class in some creative way other than a written report.  You might:

    a.    Design a descriptive brochure advertising the items and using the information to enlighten and encourage potential buyers.
    b.    Write a museum catalog description.
    c.    Write a story featuring as a main character one of the people (fictitious, of course) involved in production of the item.
    d.    Portray the story of item's production and marketing graphically through a series of sequentially organized drawings or paintings.

e. Make a tape telling the production and marketing story as interestingly as possible.

f. Write a play based on one aspect of the life of one or more persons responsible for some phase of item production and ask friends to help present it to the class.

g. Or devise your own very special way. Just remember to make your presentation as original and interesting as possible.

Extension:

An in-depth study of items manufactured in the United States and shipped to other countries would make an interesting follow-up to this activity.

METROPOLITAN MADNESS

Purpose:    After completing this activity the student should be able
            to express awareness of the uniqueness of individual
            cities and knowledge of some commonalities of all
            major metropolitan areas.

1.    Provide a variety of resource books, pictures, and other resources
      focusing on the development of metropolitan areas.  Arrange on the
      art work tables a collection of coat hangers, twigs and branches from
      trees, dowel sticks, sewing thread, yarn, ribbons, gift wrap tie,
      paper clips, straight pins, paste, many colors of construction paper,
      felt tip pens, pastel chalk, crayons, and small items from the
      classroom "Good Junk Box", such as spools, styrofoam, carpet
      and fabric scraps, small boxes, shells, artificial flowers, etc.

2.    Guide a class discussion of large cities familiar to the students
      through either real or vicarious experiences.  Ask leading questions
      such as:

      How do you define a metropolitan area?
      What do the terms residential area and commercial area
          mean?  Why do all large cities have to have both?
      What influence did access to major waterways have on
          the location of early cities?
      What factors contribute to the location of the world's major
          cities?
      Why do you find many different ethnic groups living in
          large cities of the world?
      How do life styles of people living in large cities differ
          from those of people living in small towns or rural areas?
      Why do you find so many tall buildings in large cities?

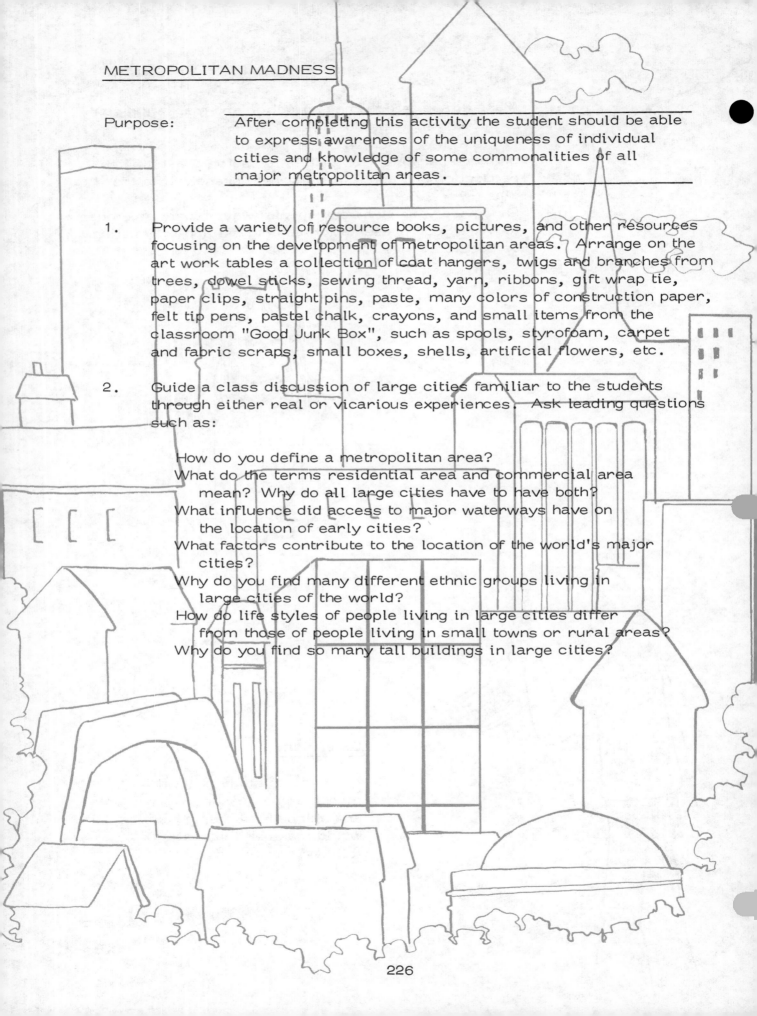

3. Culminate the discussion by asking the students to contribute to a list of the most interesting large cities in the world. Print the list on a chart or the chalk board.

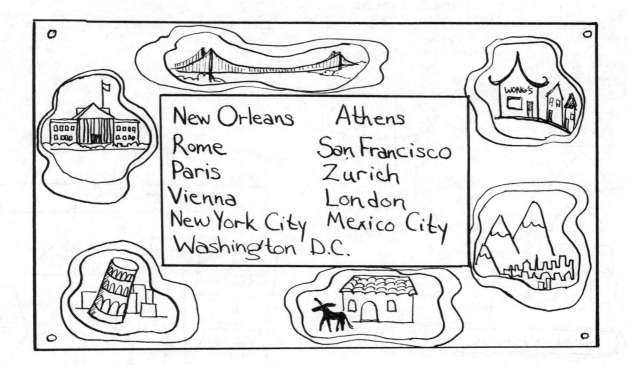

New Orleans    Athens
Rome           San Francisco
Paris          Zurich
Vienna         London
New York City  Mexico City
Washington D.C.

4. Ask each student to select the city that interests him most and follow these instructions:

(1) Use reference materials to write a factual report on the city of your choice.

(2) List at least ten important facts about the city, including information related to location, history, industry, recreation facilities, life styles of the people, government, and career, scenic and cultural advantages.

(3) Select art materials to make a mobile to portray the city. Your mobile should show at least five different and distinct phases of the city's uniqueness. Be sure your mobile is "balanced" from both physical and concept standpoints.

5. Hang the mobiles from the classroom ceiling.

6. Arrange for a follow-up discussion for students to present completed mobiles and tell why they included ideas, concepts, and information.

7. Guide the discussion to highlight common elements of all cities and unique features of each.

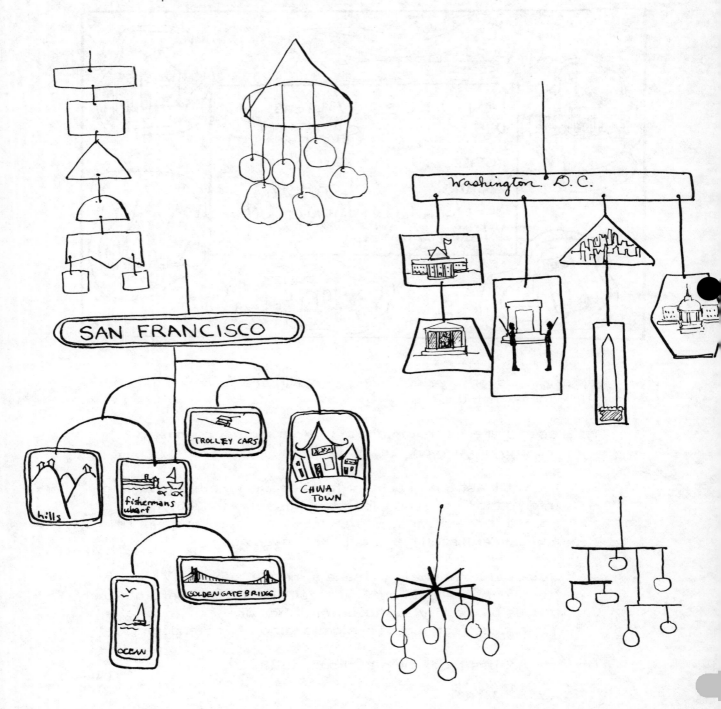

# PROJECT INTERPOL

Purpose:    After completing this activity the student should be able
to demonstrate knowledge of a variety of facts related
to world history.

1.    Prepare a copy of the following page of questions for each student.

2.    Ask students to pretend that, together, they are a special unit
of the International Police Force.  It is their job to find the
solutions to these puzzling ancient mysteries and some questions
of modern times.

3.    Provide library time and extra sets of reference books for students
to use.

4.    Ask each student to choose at least five questions, OR let them work
in pairs to answer ten questions per pair.

5.    When all "sleuthing" has been completed, ask students to sign up
by the number of one or two questions to which they will present
the solutions.  This will give the class an opportunity to hear
solutions and add any discussion necessary for each question on
the list.

Encourage students to include diagrams, illustrations, and
demonstrations in their presentations whenever possible.

Adaptation:

Ask each student to add to the list
at least one puzzling question that
he would like to have answered.
Include these in the plans for solution.

CAN YOU SOLVE THESE MYSTERIES????

?

1. Who invented money?

2. Why is 13 supposed to be an unlucky number?

3. How did slavery begin?

4. How did April Fools' Day begin?

5. Why do men tip their hats?

6. Why did the Indians sell Manhattan for $24?

7. Where was the first railroad train trip taken?

8. Was there a real King Arthur?

9. Who started the first war?

10. When did card games start?

11. Was there a real Robin Hood?

12. Why did men wear wigs long ago?

13. Why do we say "God bless you" when someone sneezes?

14. Why does traffic travel on the right side of the road in some countries and on the left in others?

15. When did the Olympic Games start?

16. Why was the Sphinx built?  How long did it take?

17. Why is a football shaped like an egg?

18. Who invented taxes?

19. How did countries get started?

20. Who made the first calendar?  The first clock?

# READ ALL ABOUT IT

Purpose:     After completing this activity the student should be able to read newspapers and news magazines critically.

1. Ask the students to contribute to a collection of various types of current newspapers and news magazines (local, state, and national daily and weekly newspapers, school and classroom papers and magazines, Weekly Readers, News Explorers, Newsweek, etc.).

2. Examine each of the newspapers and magazines within the framework of group discussion. Discuss, the title, make-up, content, cost, and availability, and try to determine the intended audience as each one is presented.

3. Ask questions such as:

   Which part of the newspaper do you read first?
   Which part does your father (mother, grandmother, boy or
        girl friend, etc.) read first?
   How important do you think the headlines are?
   Who determines what goes on the front page? What kind
        of news is usually found there?

4. Select three or more topics of current interest. List the topics on the chalk board.

5. Instruct students to form groups of three to "Read All About" one of the topics by each reading about the same topic in a different publication and comparing the information as presented in the separate articles.

6. Provide the following discussion guidelines printed on a chart or the chalk board.

When Reading a News Article you should consider:
1) The position of the author
2) The thoroughness of detail (does it tell who, when, where, + what)
3) The writing style
4) Is a bid made for sensationalism?
5) The possibility of editorial bias or opinion
6) Placement of the article
7) Evidence of "watering the news down"
8) Other influences on the manner in which the facts are presented

7. Reconvene the total group and discuss conclusions drawn by the small groups.

Extension:

A study of the history of newspapers might provide an interesting follow-up to this activity. One group of students might research and report on the first printed news accounts known to the world, going back to clay tablets in Egypt in 1450 B.C., one group on the first printed newspapers, one group on early newspapers in the United States, and another group on the evolution of newspapers around the world as we know them today. As the reports are given, attention could be drawn to common purposes and functions of newspapers through the ages.

# RED CROSS TO THE RESCUE

Purpose: After completing this activity the student should be able to express awareness of the ideals and functions of the Red Cross.

1.  Provide a large shoe box which is decorated to appear like a Red Cross First Aid kit. Place it in a center or near the front of the room.

2.  Explain to students that they are going to be introduced to one of the largest international service organizations in the world--one whose job is to help people of all nations, creeds, and colors. (More than 200,000,000 people in over one hundred countries belong to the Red Cross.)

    Wherever there is a Red Cross society, the members are committed to several basic ideas or principles.

    Write these on the board or reproduce the following page for each student. Then discuss the meaning of each principle.

3. Give students a copy of the "band-aid" page. Explain that each band-aid represents a kind of situation in which the Red Cross helps people.

4. Have students use library reference and resource materials (see Bibliography) to locate information about the ways in which the Red Cross functions to aid people in each kind of situation mentioned in the labels on the band-aids.

5. Ask students to list on each band-aid as many ways as possible that the Red Cross helps in that given kind of situation.

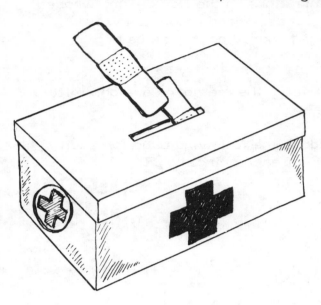

6. Cut out completed band-aids and insert them into the large First Aid kit to be reviewed and shared later.

7. Use strips of white construction paper to make arm bands. As each student completes his "band-aid" research, he takes a paper strip and makes a Red Cross arm band. On the arm band he must write one thing a young person can do to become involved with or help the Red Cross.

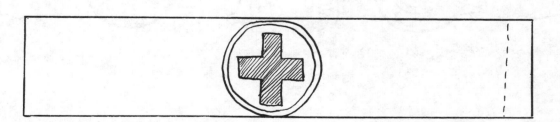

# The Ideals of the Red Cross

1.  <u>Humanity</u>.  The purpose of the Red Cross is to ease human
    suffering and to encourage health and respect for all people.
    The Red Cross works actively for understanding, friendship,
    cooperation, and peace for all people.

2.  <u>Impartiality</u>.  The Red Cross does not discriminate, or show
    favor, in any way among nations, races, religions, social
    classes, or political ideas.

3.  <u>Neutrality</u>.  The Red Cross does not take sides.

4.  <u>Independence</u>.  Although the national societies of the Red Cross
    are arms of their governments that work to help people live
    better, they must remain independent of politics in order to
    uphold the Red Cross principles.

5.  <u>Voluntary service</u>.  The Red Cross is a voluntary organization.
    It does not ever work for money or gain of any kind.

6.  <u>Unity</u>.  A nation may have only one Red Cross society.  The
    society must be open to everyone.

7.  <u>Universality</u>.  The Red Cross is a worldwide organization
    in which all the member societies work, share, and act as equals.

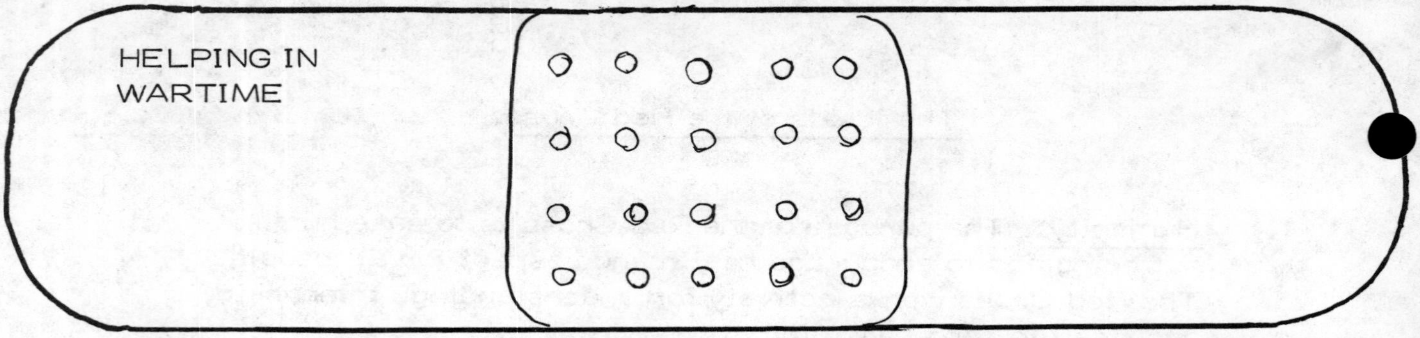

HELPING IN
WARTIME

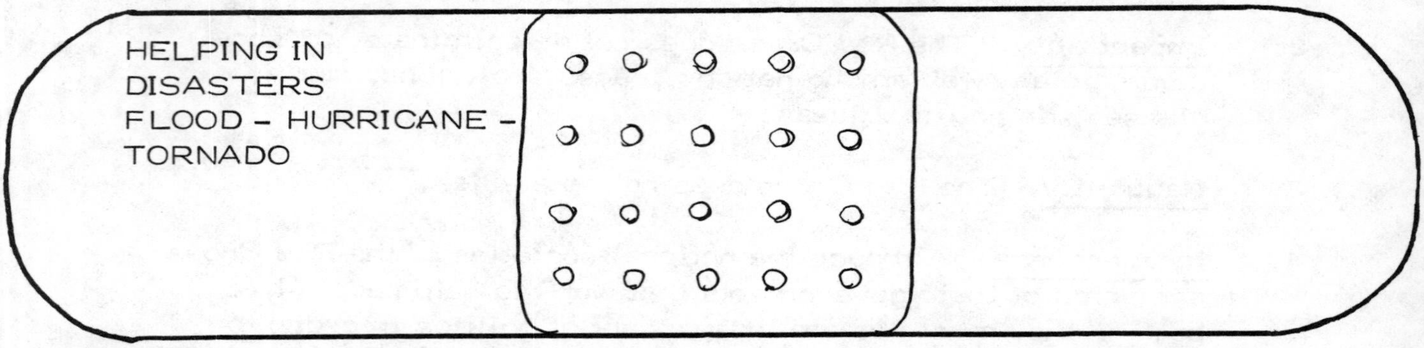

HELPING IN
DISASTERS
FLOOD — HURRICANE —
TORNADO

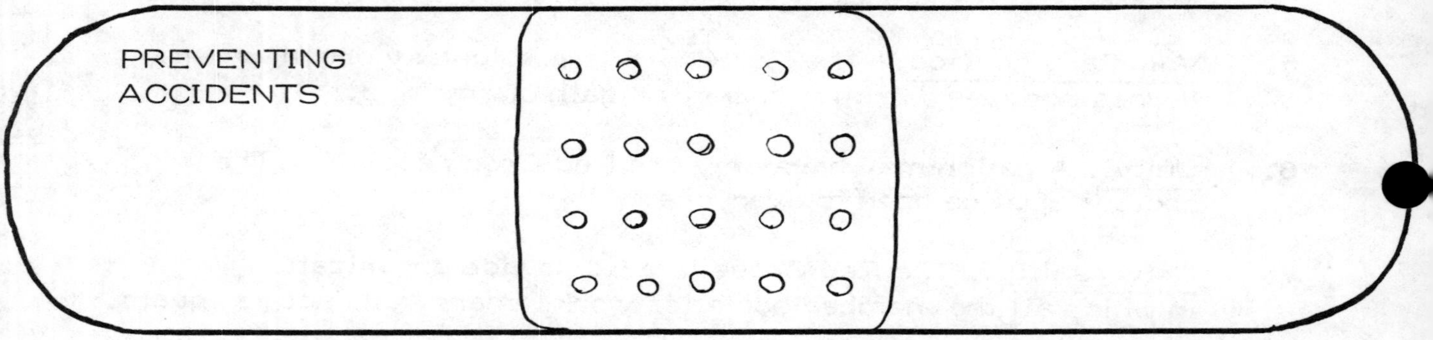

PREVENTING
ACCIDENTS

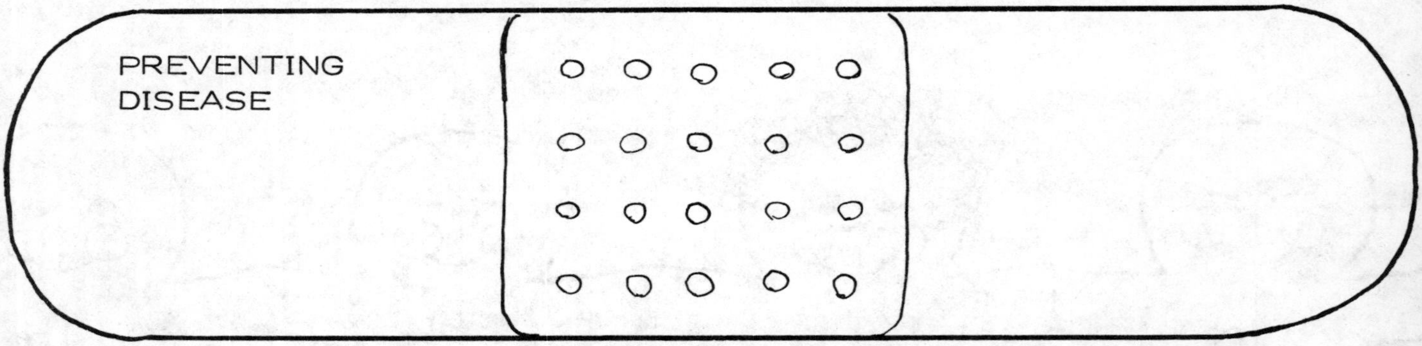

PREVENTING
DISEASE

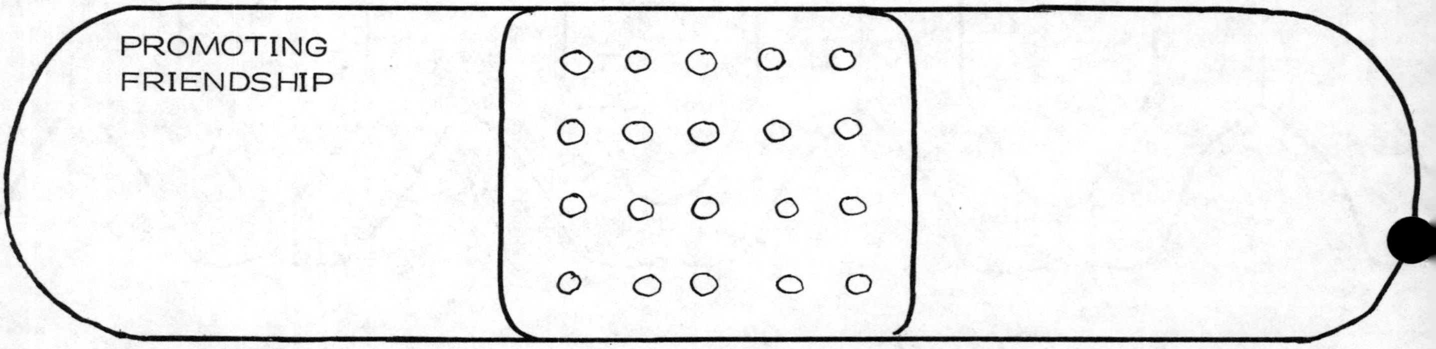

PROMOTING
FRIENDSHIP

# SALTY DOGS

Purpose: After completing this activity the student should be able to demonstrate understanding and appreciation of ocean–related careers.

1. Provide a large world map, resource books, pencils, paper, and art materials.

2. Identify the oceans of the world on the map and lead a class discussion on the location and uniqueness of each.

3. Direct students to use resource books and work in small groups to list and briefly define seafaring occupations. The listing should include each ocean site where the particular occupation takes place.

> Oceanic Occupation
> 1. Fishing
> 2. Marine Biologist
> 3. Sailor
> 4. Diver
> 5. Merchant Ship Owner
> 6. Engineer
> 7. Lighthouse Keeper

4. Make a composite listing of the occupations to be used for future student reference.

5. Ask each group to select one occupation to research in detail and present to the large group in some creative manner (a mural, skit, panel discussion, etc.).

Adaptation:

The above activity is applicable to a study of mountains, forests, or deserts.

# SIGNS OF THE TIMES

Purpose: After completing this activity the student should be able to recognize and use contemporary road and public facility signs.

1. Reproduce the Sign Work Board shown on the following page on tagboard. (Use the opaque projector to enlarge the board if desired.) Laminate the finished product or cover it with clear plastic to make it more durable.

2. Prepare an answer key with the following information:

### Signs of the Times Answer Key

3.   Label twelve clip-type clothespins with the following sign messages:

Do Not Enter      Women
No Left Turn      Men
No Trucks         First Aid
Yield             Airport
School Crossing   Handicapped
Hill              Telephone

4.   Prepare a study guide with the following instructions.

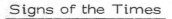

## Signs of the Times

Because so many people travel in countries other than their
own, an international sign language has been developed.  This
sign language will help travelers all over the world to use roads
and public facilities in countries where they do not read or
speak the native language.  These signs have been used in
Europe for several years and are now being introduced in
more and more parts of the United States.

Study the signs on the "Signs of the Times" work board.  Take
the clothespins from the box and clip them to the section of the
board representing the sign message printed on the clothespin.

When you have finished, use the answer key you will find in the
folder to check your answers.

5.   Place the work board, clothespins, answer key, and reference
books (see Bibliography) in a learning center or independent work
area to be used as a free time activity.

Adaptation:

More mature students might enjoy
and profit from researching the
history of the international sign
language and/or using one of the
signs as the theme for a creative
writing project.

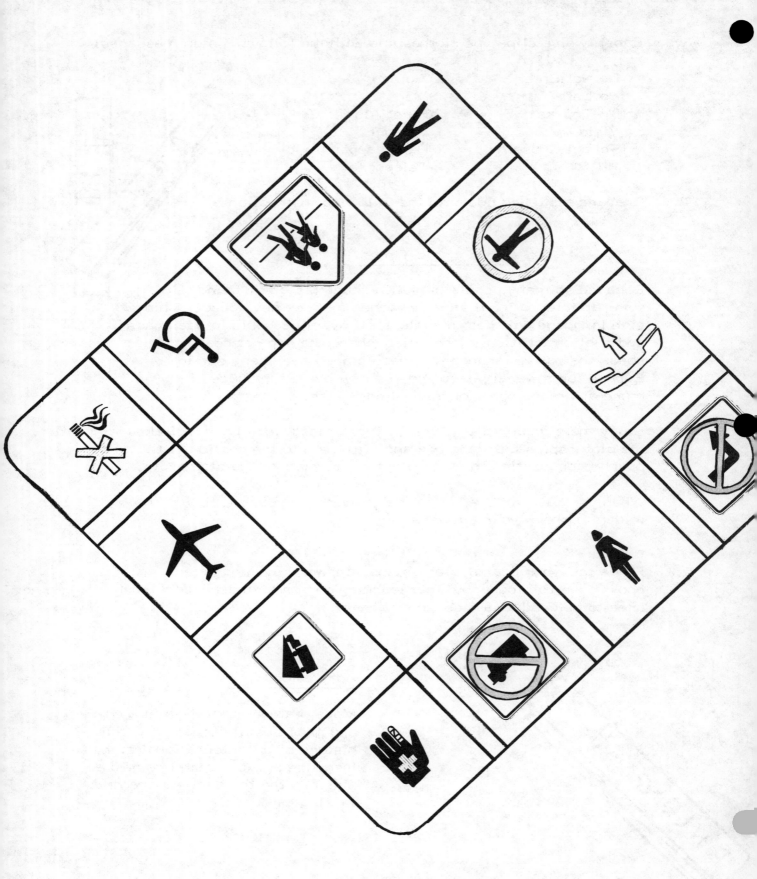

240

## SOME CALL IT MURDER

**Purpose:**  After completing this activity the student should be able to identify some of the animals of the world that are in danger of extinction and to express positive awareness of steps being taken to preserve them.

1.  Provide a wide variety of resource materials dealing with animals in danger of becoming extinct.  This collection should include reference books, pictures, magazines, and film strips (see Bibliography).

2.  Instruct the students to use the resource materials on their own to read about the problem of endangered animal species and to plan an independent study of one particular animal that they would like to campaign to save.

3.  Distribute copies of the outline for independent study on the following page.

4.  Emphasize the importance of thorough research, careful organization of factual information, and creative presentation of the ideas and conservation concepts.

5.  Designate a time for sharing independent activities in a group setting.

6.  Present the names and addresses of organizations devoted to the preservation of animals in danger of extinction.  Ask each student to write a letter to one or more of these organizations as part of the individual project:

World Wildlife Fund
910 – 17th Street, N. W.
Washington, D. C.  20006

International Union of Conservation
 of Nature and Natural Resources
1110 Murges
Vaud, Switzerland

National Audubon Society
950 Third Avenue
New York, New York  10022

SOME CALL IT MURDER – Independent Study Plan

Name of Animal: _____

Animal's Natural Habitat: _____
_____

Reference Sources to be used: _____
_____
_____

Facts About the Animal: _____
_____
_____
_____

Steps that can be taken to protect the animal: _____
_____
_____
_____

Plan for reporting to the class: _____
_____
_____
_____

Organization to contact: _____
_____
_____

# TELL-TALE GAMES

Purpose: | After completing this activity the student should be able to demonstrate his awareness that the children's games of a given culture are representative of the geography, values, practices, and traditions of that group of people.

1.  Write on the chalk board the names of the following games and the countries from which they originated.

| | |
|---|---|
| Eagle and Goats | Switzerland |
| Thumping Sticks | Africa |
| The Game of the Stone | Portugal |
| The Troll Head | Denmark |
| Portrait Painter | Japan |

2.  Explain to the students that you will assist them in reading and following directions for playing the five games.

    Note:  All students may participate in all five games, played one at a time, or students may be divided into smaller groups and each group may play one game, observed by the remainder of the class.

3.  Let the students observe the playing of all five games.  After this, conduct a discussion of children's games as representative of a given culture by asking students to conjecture about how these particular five games came to be popular in their place of origin. How do they relate to the people, the geography, the values, the practices, the traditions of these lands? Name American children's games that are representative of our culture and some which were borrowed from other cultures and tell where they came from and why.

## EAGLE AND GOATS

This game from Switzerland involves 7-15 players, usually 6-10 years of age, and is enjoyed by boys and girls alike.

The game begins with a player selected to be the Eagle, the others being Goats. The Goats pretend to graze in the pasture when the Eagle, swooping with "wings" outstretched, appears to be trying to catch them in his "claws". The Goats must quickly guess which of them is the Eagle's intended prey and hide him in a circle. Should they guess correctly, the Eagle flies off and they resume grazing. If not, the Eagle announces the name of the one he's after. If this Goat isn't quickly hidden in a circle, the Eagle catches him and drags him off. This is repeated until all but one of the Goats have been caught. The last Goat is the Eagle for the next game.

# THUMPING STICKS
## (Chigoro Danda)

This game, popular with the African children, involves 3-10 children, only three of whom actively participate at one time while the others watch, clap and sing until one of the main participants fails and is replaced. The three main players use three sticks (poles) about three inches think and five feet long, two of which are laid parallel to each other as base bars, approximately four feet apart. The third bar is used as a cross bar over them about in the center. One player sits at either end of the cross bar and the third stands between the parallel bars, straddling the cross bar.

The two seated players lift the cross bar simultaneously and strike it rhythmically against the base sticks. The player in the center hops rhythmically on the cross bar each time it strikes the base bars. While the rhythm starts slowly, it speeds up and the player in the middle must hop and step on the cross bar at the same pace as the rhythm. If he fails, he is replaced by one of the observers. The inactive players (observers) may either stand or sit in a circle and sing/clap hands to the rhythm of the "sticks".

The African children sing while they clap: "Aiye chigoro danda chigoro." The words are descriptive of the sound (chigoro) made by the pole (danda).

## THE GAME OF THE STONE
### (Jogo da Pedra)

This out-of-doors game from Portugal involves 2-15 players, ranging from 10-14 years of age.

The players find nine flat and nine round stones, each about as large as an apple.  They place the flat stones in a row with the round stones on top of them.  The players, in turn, take nine small stones, each large enough to be held in the palm of the hand.  They stand about fifteen feet from the row of stones and begin throwing at them.  One point is scored for each round stone that is knocked off its flat base.  The individual scores are counted up and the player with the highest score is the winner.

## THE TROLL HEAD

This game from Denmark might be played in or out of doors and as many as 25 may participate.  (Good game for 6-10 year old age group)

A huge troll's head (children-eating monster) is drawn on the ground with a stick in dirt or chalk on sidewalk or floor.  The players get situated along the outline and the leader gives a shriek.  At this point the children try to push one another off the line.  Any child who is pushed inside the head has been "eaten" and is out of the game.  All the players' arms are folded over their chests while pushing, using their bodies alone to push with.  The players may "gang up" on one another if they wish. The last player to remain on the line is the winner.

PORTRAIT PAINTER

This is a fun game for 6–10 year olds, involving anywhere from 10 to 30 players.

Three to five children are selected as Artists and they are situated before the rest of the group with large white papers tied over their faces – completely covering them. They are equipped with brushes (such as those used in Japanese writing) dipped into ink, with which they simultaneously paint their own faces on the paper, following directions given by the leader. Instructions may be "draw the left ear, the right eye, the mouth, etc." until all the facial features are completed. The artists are then presented (in parade fashion) before they may see their own faces. (The paper must be adequately stiff to stay flat and prevent the pressure of the brush from being felt through it.)

# TERMINOLOGY SPEEDWAY

Purpose:   After completing this activity the student should be able
to locate and use definitions of social studies words
and terms.

1.   Prepare a game board from tagboard to represent a race track
with twenty-two sections.

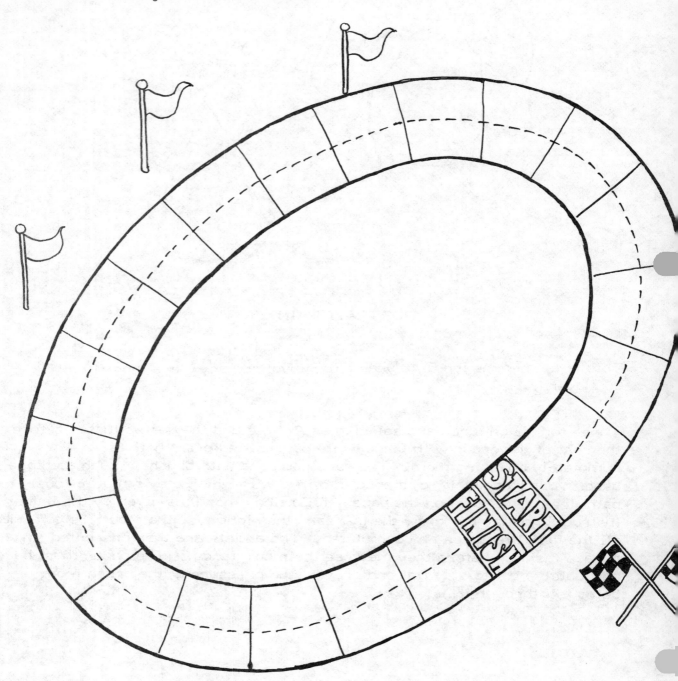

2. Use sixty 3 x 5" index cards to make game cards. Print one of the words on the following page on each card.

3. Provide toy race cars and dictionaries for each player.

4. Place the game materials and a chart with the following player instructions in a learning center or free-time activity setting.

## Player Directions

1. This game is for two to four players.

2. Each player selects a race car.

3. The cards are placed face down in the center of the race track. The top card is turned up, and each player attempts to locate the word in the dictionary.

4. The first player to locate the word reads the definition aloud and moves his car one space ahead on the game board.

5. The first player to cross the "finish line" wins the game.

## Word List

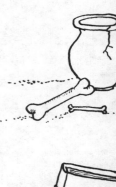

heritage
culture
globe
hemisphere
latitude
longitude
equator
compass
ocean
seaport
import
export
continental shelf
continental divide
continent
desert
amendment
law
legislator
legislature
election
impeachment
NATO
inauguration
jurisdiction
juror
judicial
Supreme Court
forestry
economy

anthropology
sociology
history
geography
atlas
cartology
community
tradition
ethnic
racial
partisan
nation
ballot
immigration
citizenship
communication
municipality
country
international
environment
manufacture
democracy
population
dictatorship
treaty
civil
frontier
responsibility
colonial
conservation

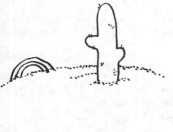

250

# THREE-MINUTE LOCATIONS

Purpose:      After completing this activity the student should be able to identify land formations on a map or globe.

1.    Glue the following page on poster board and cut apart to form game cards. Laminate or cover the game cards with plastic.

2.    Any number of students may play this game.

3.    Provide a large world map or globe, three-minute timer, pointer, bowl filled with tokens (beans, pebbles, or colored circles of paper), the game cards, and the following instructions.

## Player Directions

1.    Players sit in a circle with the world map or globe in the center of the circle.

2.    The game cards are placed face down near the map or globe.

3.    The first player draws a card, turns the three-minute timer "on", reads the word on the card, and picks up the pointer. The player then tries to point to three specific examples of the subject on the card as quickly as possible.

4.    If the player is able to do so in three minutes or less he or she takes three tokens from the bowl. If only one or two are found the player takes no tokens.

5.    The game continues until one player has twenty-one tokens and is declared the winner.

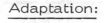

Adaptation:

The rules of this game may be adjusted for younger or less mature students by requiring only one location rather than three. More capable students might be asked to give one fact about each location or the time limit might be shortened.

Rivers

Oceans

Mountains

Forests

Islands

Lakes

Deserts

Jungles

TOOL TALK

Purpose:     After completing this activity the student should be able
             to identify a variety of common tools and to express
             awareness of their influences on everyday life.

1.   Fill a tool box or a shopping bag
     with a collection of common tools
     such as a hammer, paint brush,
     saw, paring knife, scissors,
     tweezers, fork, etc.

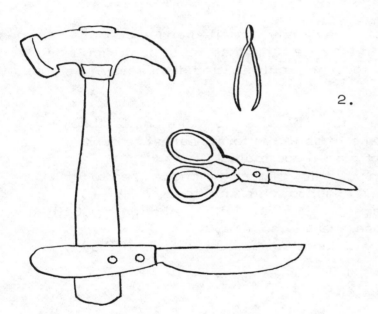

2.   Fill a like container with objects
     available from the natural
     environment that might be
     substituted to do the jobs of the
     tools if the tools were not
     available.  This collection might
     include sharp and blunt edged
     rocks, sticks, tree bark, strong
     grasses and/or supple tree
     branches, hunks of wood, sea
     shells, etc.

3.   Place a board and a nail, a potato, carrot, or cucumber, a heavy
     tree branch, and a length of fabric or leather on a table in the center
     of the circle.

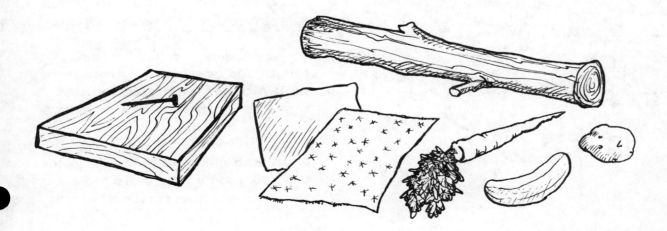

4.  Place the tools on one side of the table and the objects from nature on the other. Ask one student to come to the table and select one or more objects from the natural object group to use to peel and slice the vegetable; one student to select a natural object to drive the nail into the board; one student to use a natural object to separate the tree branch into three parts; and one student to divide the fabric or leather in half. As each of the demonstrations is carried out, encourage students in the group to make suggestions or comments as to procedure or task completion.

5.  Ask each experimenter to select a tool from the collection to use to complete the task as the second phase of the activity.

6.  Refer to the list of tools previously compiled and encourage comments relevant to situations in everyday life that would be difficult or even impossible without the tools in a culminating discussion. Ask questions such as:

> Can you name at least ten tools used to make one textbook?
> How long would it take to go to the town nearest to ours
>     without the use of man-made tools?
> How many tools can you think of that the cooks used to
>     prepare lunch in our school cafeteria today?
> How would the barber cut your hair without the tools usually used?
> What tools do you use every school day?
> How or what would you substitute for these tools if they were
>     not available?

Adaptation or Extension:

Objects used, demonstrations, and length and depth of discussion might be limited or expanded to meet students' abilities and interests.

Class or individual booklets, murals, or dioramas could be made to trace the development of tools from early times to the present.

# A TOUCH OF GLASS

Purpose: | After completing this activity the student should be able to demonstrate increased understanding of the historic and economic significance of glass.

1. Arrange a collection of glass objects to serve as motivation for this activity. Include decorative as well as utilitarian objects (laboratory test tubes, drinking glasses, glass jewelry, cosmetic containers, soda bottles, blown glass objects, etc.) Lead the discussion to focus attention on the number of glass items used every day, the cost of glass, the process required to make glass, and other topics in keeping with the students' knowledge and maturity.

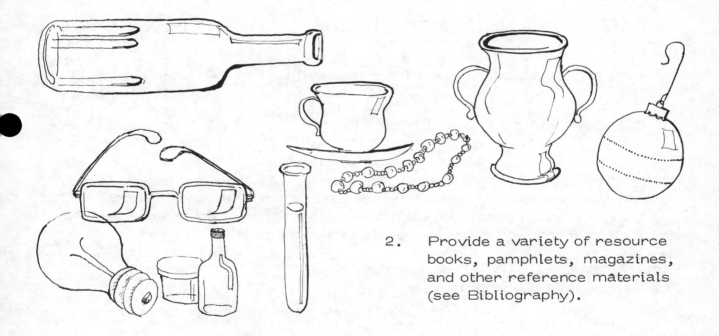

2. Provide a variety of resource books, pamphlets, magazines, and other reference materials (see Bibliography).

3. Divide the class into five groups and ask each group to be responsible for researching one of the following topics:

    (1) History of glass
    (2) Process used to make glass
    (3) Aesthetic uses of glass through the ages
    (4) Ways in which we depend on glass in our daily lives
    (5) Creative ways glass might be used in the future

4.    Provide mural paper, pastel chalk, and black felt tip markers.
      Divide the paper into five sections.

5.    Ask each student group to plan and draw a pictorial account of
      the research findings related to the assigned topic.

The completed mural should provide an attractive and informative
documentation of the history and uses of glass through the ages,
and should serve to direct attention to another of the many scientific
and economic processes people today tend to take for granted.

6.    Take a field trip to visit a glass
      blower at work or to a specialty
      shop featuring glass objects as
      reinforcement for this learning
      experience.

Adaptation:

The basic plan for this activity
could be used to study similar
products such as bricks, plastic,
or steel.

# TABLES OF FABLES, FOLKLORE AND MORE

Purpose: After completing this activity the student should be able to relate stories, rhymes, and riddles from folklore and legend to the customs, beliefs, and character of a given people, time, and place.

1. Make available to students many, many volumes of folk tales, stories, legends, rhymes, and riddles (see Bibliography). Ask them to spend at least fifteen minutes to one hour reading and enjoying as many of them as possible.

2. Set aside at least twenty minutes or more of class time each day for several days to read aloud short folk stories and poems which come from a variety of geographical areas. Students might be asked to guess the regions where the stories were born.

3. Ask students to work individually or in pairs to create a folk story, legend, poem, or collection of riddles which reflect their own modern-day life and geographical locations after they have had ample opportunity to read and enjoy many selections.

   Caution them to be sure that their final products contain their own wit, humor, values, customs, environment, and a lot of their imagination.

4. Help students get started on their creative efforts by sharing with them the following list of possibilities:

   Stories of talking animals          Scary and mock-scary stories
   How and why stories                 Legends of heroes and heroines
   Truckster stories                   Chain tales
   Nonsense tales                      Tales of wonder and enchantment
   Tall tales                          Alphabet rhyme
   Riddle stories                      Autograph album rhymes
   Fables                              Teasing rhymes
   Parables                            Jump-rope and bounce-ball rhymes

5. Provide a time for sharing stories and rhymes. Allow students to put some of them on tape for use in the listening center. Place others in the reading center to be enjoyed in free time.

# TRIVIA TRIANGLE

Purpose: After completing this activity the student should be able to use the encyclopedia to locate facts related to a specific subject.

1. Cover a potato chip or oatmeal box with contact paper, tissue paper, or paint. Fill it with popsicle sticks on which topics in keeping with the students' social studies interests have been printed. For example:

| | |
|---|---|
| South America | Washington, D. C. |
| The United Nations | Civil War |
| Atlantic Ocean | The Development of Aviation |
| Christopher Columbus | The Industrial Revolution |
| Abraham Lincoln | Carrie Nation |

2. Ask the students to assist in cutting triangular-shaped banners in different sizes from pastel-colored construction paper.

3. Provide felt tip markers in as many colors as possible and reference books such as encyclopedias, dictionaries, and social studies texts.

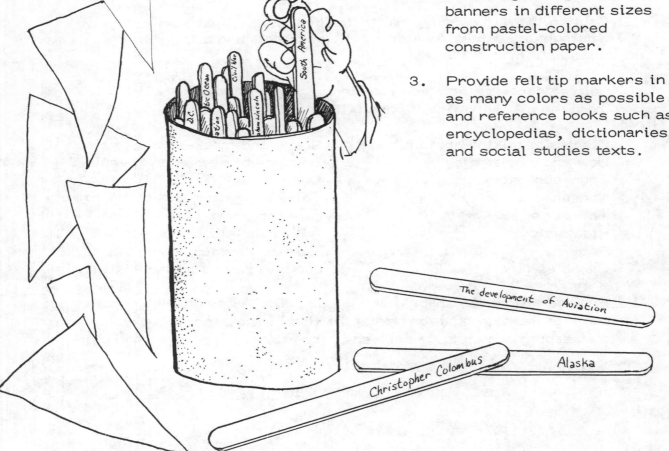

4.  Direct students to take one popsicle stick (without looking at it) and use the reference books to find at least three previously unknown (to them) facts concerning the printed subject.

5.  Allow the students to select a paper banner to decorate by printing the facts artistically with the felt tip markers.

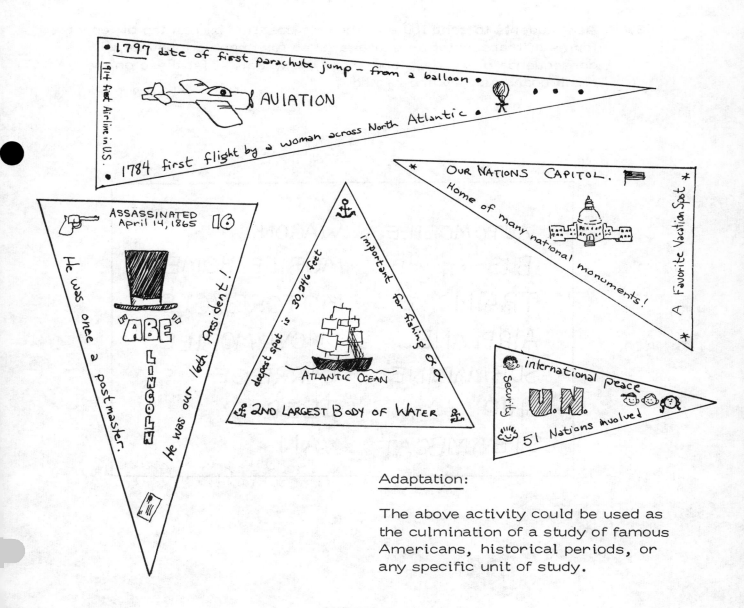

Adaptation:

The above activity could be used as the culmination of a study of famous Americans, historical periods, or any specific unit of study.

# WHEELING AROUND

Purpose:     After completing this activity the student should be able to pictorially express understanding of the development of several different forms of transportation.

1.     Provide a collection of resource materials dealing with the history and development of transportation, felt tip pens, paper brads, and copies of the "Wheeling Around" work sheet on the following page.

2.     Present verbally accounts from the reference books of the early development of the wheel and of the changes brought about by its use. Guide the ensuing discussion to direct attention to the wheel's adaptation to moving people and objects from place to place, and its continuing influence on life styles, industry, and historical progress.

3.     Ask students to contribute to the conversation by naming different forms of transportation that are taken for granted today as a consequence of the development of the wheel. List these on the chalk board as they are named.

| | |
|---|---|
| AUTOMOBILE | WAGON |
| BUS | MOBILE HOME |
| TRAIN | MOTORCYCLE |
| AIRPLANE | SNOW MOBILE |
| SUBMARINE | CARRIAGE |
| SHIP | JEEP |
| STEAMBOAT | VAN |

4. Instruct each student to construct a "Wheeling Around" wheel in the following manner:

   (1)    Present the development and use of one means of transportation in picture form by using the twelve spaces provided inside the wheel.

   (2)    Use resource materials to help you plan the sequence of pictures very carefully <u>before</u> you begin drawing.

   (3)    You may use only three words in any way you choose to help your pictures tell the story. You may use each of the words anywhere you wish in the design but they may be used only once.

   (4)    Cut out your completed wheel and paste it on a circle of tagboard of the same size. Push a paper brad through the center of the wheel to be used to turn the wheel.

5. Prepare a bulletin board by cutting letters from black construction paper to form the title "Wheeling Around". Pin sheets of black construction paper to the board to form mats from the completed wheels. Instruct the students to pin their wheels to the mats by using only one pin in the center of the wheel so that the wheels will turn.

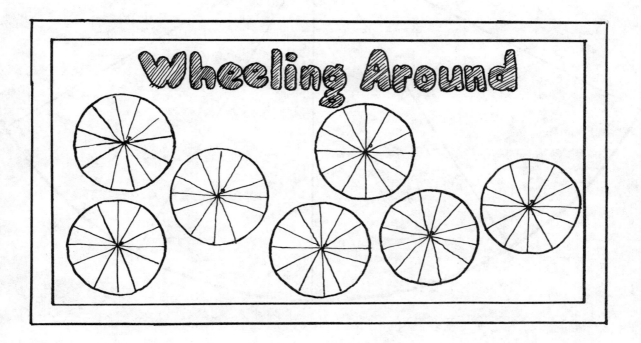

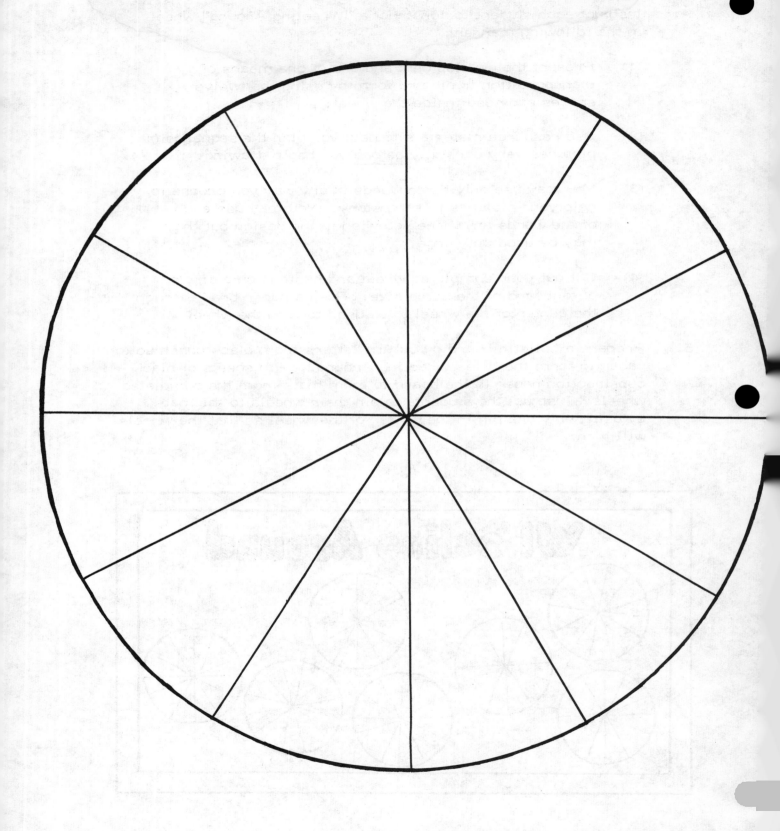

# WHO KNOWS THE NEWS?

Purpose: After completing this activity the student should be able to demonstrate awareness of names prominent in current news events.

1. Provide for each pupil a duplicated identification sheet with space for the following information:

| Name | News Personality | A Line of Identification |
|------|------------------|--------------------------|
|      |                  |                          |

2. Inform students a day or two in advance that they will be required to assume the identity of a prominent "name in the news". Ask them to prepare themselves by listening to and reading as many current news reports as possible and making a first, second, and third choice of persons they will be.

3. Make a list of these choices and assign each student to a role so as not to duplicate names which will be represented.

4. Ask each student upon arrival to use a felt tip marker to write his news personality identity on the bottom of his shoe on the appointed day.

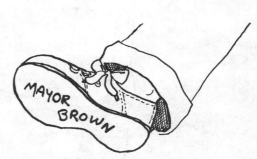

5. Give each student a copy of the prepared information form.

6. Have each individual complete his information form by listing each of his classmate's names in the first column, that person's news personality name in the second column, and a single phrase or sentence in the third column that tells why that person is prominent in the news.

7.  Let the students obtain this information by employing a "20 questions" type technique. Only questions which may be answered with "yes" or "no" or "I don't know" may be asked. (Of course, it is expected that all VIPs will always tell the truth!)

8.  When a person guesses a name correctly, the "discovered" personality verifies it by showing him the bottom of his shoe.

9.  Continue the game over a limited time period or throughout the day until all identities have been discovered.

Guarantee: By the end of the day most class members will be well aware of newsworthy names and the reasons for their prominence in the news!

WHY WAR?

Purpose: After completing this activity the student should be able to demonstrate his understanding of the ideologies and elements involved in war.

1.  Provide a copy of the following page to each student. Ask him to give careful thought to each statement before completing it with his own words and ideas.

2.  Instruct the student to mark the box by each number with either a T or a K after all statements have been completed. T indicates that he thinks the statement he has just completed is true. K indicates that he feels he knows for sure that it is true.

3.  Provide time for students to gather in small groups and discuss their answers after they have all had time to complete their inventories.

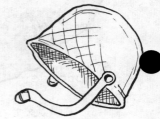

THINK AND KNOW INVENTORY

Subject: _____ WAR _____

Think or Know?

☐     1.     A good definition of war is _____

_____

_____

_____

☐     2.     War is caused by _____

_____

_____

☐     3.     War is _____ necessary for the following

reasons: _____

_____

_____

☐     4.     If the voting people in a democracy could decide one thing

about war, it should be _____

_____

_____

☐     5.     War should be fought only _____

_____

_____

_____

6. [ ] _____ is/are always hurt by war.

7. [ ] War can be fought in many ways:

   (1) _____

   (2) _____

   (3) _____

8. [ ] A democratic government at war is _____

   a totalitarian government at war.

9. [ ] The people most hurt by war are _____

   _____

10. [ ] Something students can do about war is _____

   _____

   _____

   _____

   _____

11. [ ] I _____ war could be avoided _____

   _____

   _____

   _____

   _____

# WORLD ON A STRING

Purpose: After completing this activity the student should be able to name and locate continents and oceans on a globe.

1. Provide a balloon, tempera paint, paint brushes, scissors, paste, newspaper strips, string, black felt tip pens, and a copy of the continents on the following page for each student.

2. Make art supplies available after a discussion of the globe, and give the following directions:

    (1) Blow up your balloon and tie it with a string approximately 18" long.

    (2) Use the newspaper strips and paste to cover the balloon completely. It will take at least three layers of newspaper stripping to form a sturdy paper ball.

    (3) Paint the entire surface with blue tempera paint. Leave to dry overnight.

    (4) Cut the continents from the work page provided and paste in their appropriate places on the globe. Use a felt tip pen to label the oceans.

    (5) Relax and enjoy your own "world on a string" and learn more about the real world of which you are a part.

# notes .....

APPENDIX

# SOCIAL STUDIES ADVENTURELAND

A well balanced reading program will help you to learn more about yourself, the world around you and the people who share the world with you. The Social Studies Adventureland map on the next page will serve as your guide as you plan and carry out this kind of reading program. Begin the journey by reading about people and events close to home and follow the directions to expand your knowledge and understanding of the bigger world beyond your front door.

(1) As you add the books specified by the map directions to your reading record, color the symbol attached to each stop.

(2) Use the accompanying work sheet to record the title, author, and date of completion for each book.

(3) Search the library shelves carefully for the most interesting books you can find and take all the time you need to finish them.

(4) Look for good illustrations, helpful glossaries, charts and graphs, and suggestions for other books on the same subject.

(5) List new words and terms you don't understand and look them up for future reference.

(6) Feel free to read more books than called for if you get really excited about any particular area.

When you are all finished, use your crayons to finish illustrating the Social Studies Adventureland map.

# Social Studies Adventure Land
## Reading Record

Book     Author     Date Finished

1.

2.

3.

4.

5.

6.

7.

8.

9.

10.

11.

12.

13.

14.

15.

16.

17.

18.

19.

20.

21.

22.

23.

24.

25.

Home Sweet Home
1 Book

To Get Started
1 Book

Finding New Friends
1 Book

Community or Town
2 Books

1 Book to move on!

Moving Out
school, church, relatives.
1 Book

Take a Giant Step to the World Beyond
3 Books for the journey.

EVERYTHING YOU ALWAYS WANTED TO KNOW ABOUT YOUR STATE (BUT WERE AFRAID TO ASK)

Find out about your state.
1 Book

BEWARE OF THE BOG !!

Don't Bog Down!
1 Book

Proud to be American!
2 Books.

Now the Nation
2 Books

Time to Broaden Horizons.
3 Books.

One for the road.
1 Book

The Whole Wide World
4 Books

Who knows maybe you will go to the moon.
1 BOOK

You've arrived in Social Studies Adventure Land!
treat yourself to a good book.

275

## TO THE TEACHER

The following pages were created to provide opportunity for young students to look carefully at themselves and their own feelings and at the other young people and adults with whom they live. Used properly, they can be useful in achieving some of the following goals:

(1) Causing students to examine WHY and HOW people build relationships
(2) Bringing about awareness that different people are attracted to different qualities in other people
(3) Understanding that different people meet different needs in the same person
(4) Helping students to identify personal attributes of themselves and others
(5) Understanding how the characteristics of one person complement those of another
(6) Helping students differentiate between good and poor reasons for making choices
(7) Bringing about awareness that visual impact strongly influences opinion, perhaps more so than written description

How to use these pages:

Provide a copy of the following pages for each student. Give little or no direction except to set a serious tone for the activity. Merely ask students to read the descriptions of the six students and three adults and answer carefully and thoughtfully the questions that follow.

After answer sheets have been completed, divide students into small groups of five or six to discuss their answers. (Asking one group of this kind to conduct its discussion in front of the entire class might be beneficial.) Concentrate on reasons WHY students made their choices and ask them to consider how their own feelings and personalities affected their choices.

Extending Activities:

(1) Choose one or two of your friends and tell why they are good friends for you.
(2) Design an imaginary super-friend who would be just perfect for you.
(3) Describe an ideal mother or father for yourself.
(4) Identify your favorite teacher. Tell what makes that teacher a good teacher for you.
(5) Name three or four people who would choose you for a friend and tell why.
Open-ended statements might be provided for this activity, such as:

_____ likes me because I _____
_____ would choose to work with me because _____
_____ would choose to be on my team because _____
I am good at _____ for other people.
Something my mother enjoys about me is _____
_____ wouldn't get along with me because _____

MEET THE GANG!

Think about each question and answer it carefully.  Be
ready to explain the reason for each choice you have made.

1.  Which kid is most like you?  _____

2.  Which is least like you?  _____

3.  Which one would be a good friend for you?  _____

4.  Which person would choose you as a friend?  _____

5.  Choose two persons to work with you in preparing a Social Studies report.

    _____ and _____

6.  With which person would you discuss a problem or share a secret?  _____

7.  Who would you choose for a partner on a camping trip?  _____

8.  Which people in this group would you like to invite to your next birthday party?

    _____

9.  Whom would you choose to help you build a go-cart?  _____

10.  Which person would be a good friend for Kris?  _____

11.  Which person would be a good friend for Cindy?  _____

12.  Which two people might not get along well on the same team?

    _____ and _____

13.  Who would be a good partner to work on a science experiment with Randy?  _____

14.  Which two people would probably work well together at planning and running a party?

    _____ and _____

ABOUT THE ADULTS...

1.  Which adult would you choose for a friend?  _____

2.  Which adult would you choose for a parent?  _____

3.  Which would you choose for a teacher?  _____

4.  Which would you choose for a leader on a hiking trip?  _____

5.  Who would be a good teacher for Scott?  _____

6.  Who would be a good teacher for Cindy?  _____

7.  Who would be a good teacher for Tammy?  _____

8.  Describe someone who would be a good friend for Miss Mills.  _____

    _____

Cindy is tall and a little heavy for her age. She is usually quiet—especially around a large group of people. She gets embarrassed and cries when she makes a mistake in front of people. She would rather write things down than tell them. She likes to write stories and poems. Cindy is serious and careful about her schoolwork and does extra projects whenever she can. She loves horses and art and is very good at drawing animals. She likes to do things for other people.

Tammy likes people, and people seem to like her. She listens to others respectfully and never gossips about them. She is small and neat and has lots of energy. She laughs a lot. She likes music and little kids. Tammy is not afraid to try new things. She works and works at something new and just won't give up. She likes to do things on her own and is good at convincing people to do things her way. Her best subject is science and she is a good softball player.

Kris has a good sense of humor and tells the funniest jokes. He likes to be around people and see them laugh. He knows a lot about animals and nature. Kris talks about things he learns, but he doesn't like to do written work because it is hard for him. He has lots of ideas for things to do and plans projects carefully before he starts. Kris does not feel very well in gym class or when playing most sports. He is happiest when he can build and fix things.

278

# MEET THE GANG!

Lori is outgoing. She talks to lots of people and
has lots of friends. Lori doesn't like math.
Sometimes she feels sick to her stomach when
it's math time. She's good at reading and likes to
read aloud to people. She talks very easily in
front of the group. Lori has pretty clothes, a
swimming pool, and a big allowance, and she
shares them all with her friends. She is good at
organizing games and getting people together to work.
Sometimes she is bossy and gets grouchy when
things don't go her way.

Randy is quiet and keeps his thoughts and
feelings to himself. He likes to be alone.
Lots of times he daydreams in school
and doesn't listen to lessons. Randy
does listen well to other people. When
someone is feeling bad, he seems to
know what to say to make them feel better.
He is afraid to try new things in school.
He knows a lot about photography and
sailboats. Randy is the best pitcher
on his little league team and is a really
good sport in games.

Scott is the leader of a big group of boys
who like sports. He is the fastest runner
in his grade. He tells the other boys what
to do and always runs the team. Sometimes
he loses his temper and gets kicked out of
games. Scott is very generous. He gives
away toys and money and candy to his
friends. Lots of girls and boys want to be
his friend. He is really good at math.
In school, he doesn't like to sit still. He
has a hard time finishing what he starts. When the teacher tries to make
him do his work carefully, he argues. Sometimes he cries when things
don't go right. He is very clever at making up fun games––and at getting
out of work. He is a very good artist.

Mr. Cohen is a short, heavy, jolly man who laughs and smiles a lot. He has a happy loud voice and is always telling funny stories. He is often starting something new and interesting for kids to do. He wants kids to do lots of things by themselves and always asks them to help make decisions about how to do it. He is usually right there to help when he is needed. He is very patient and sensitive to other people's problems. Mr. Cohen is a good cartoonist and he likes to build treehouses and swings and spaceships.

Mr. Newcomb is strong and tall and a good athlete. He loves to rough-house with kids and teach them new games. He teases a lot. He reads mystery stories and tells spooky tales. When you're working with Mr. Newcomb he sets firm rules and everybody is afraid to break them. He explains exactly what to do and gets a little mean if it is not done right. He thinks there is a time to play and a time to settle down with no messing around. Mr. Newcomb likes to paint. He sells some of his pictures. He teaches swimming at the YMCA.

Miss Mills is plump and pretty. She has a soft voice and seems very serious, but her eyes always smile. She explains things carefully to kids and answers all their questions. She makes them try new things and do them on their own. She is very strict about finishing what you start. She plays guitar very well and likes to sing. She knows how to fly a plane and she used to be a weather forecaster.

STUDY GUIDE – Primary

Getting To Know A Famous Person
_____

Name _____

Where did this person live? _____

When did this person live? _____

What was this person's home like? _____

_____

_____

Tell something interesting that happened to this person as a child.

_____

_____

_____

What were this person's parents like? _____

_____

_____

_____

How was this person's life different from yours?

School _____

_____

Clothes _____

_____

Playtime _____

_____

Family life _____

_____

Tell a good or happy thing that happened to this person. _____

_____

_____

Tell a bad or sad thing that happened to this person. _____

_____

_____

What is something this person did that you would like to do?

_____

_____

_____

Why do people remember this person? _____

_____

_____

_____

STUDY GUIDE – Intermediate

<u>Getting To Know A Famous Person</u>

Name _____

Dates this person lived _____ to _____

Place(s) of Residence _____

_____

_____


Background Information:

Describe Home.                    _____

_____

_____

Describe Parents.                 _____

_____

_____

Tell something about this         _____
person's childhood.
_____

_____


Tell how this person's life was different from yours.  (Include thoughts
about school life, clothing, hobbies and recreation, entertainment,
family life, etc.)


_____

_____

_____

_____

_____

_____

_____

Tell one important thing that happened to this person when he was young that may have contributed to his becoming a famous person.

_____

_____

_____

_____

Tell a sad or unpleasant incident from this person's life.  Do you feel this occasion helped to "build" this person's character?

_____

_____

_____

Name at least three qualities possessed by this person which you would like to possess also, and tell why:

1. _____  Why? _____

2. _____       _____

3. _____       _____

Describe three or more significant contributions made by this person.

_____

_____

_____

_____

_____

_____

_____

_____

ALL ABOUT A COUNTRY
(Outline for survey of a country)

Name _____

This survey is all about the country of _____

Part I     <u>Its Geography--What the Land Looks Like</u>
(Draw or trace below a small outline map of the country
to show its relative shape, size, and location.  On the
lines describe in simple words or a short paragraph
what kind or kinds of land are found there.)

Description of the land: _____

_____

_____

287

Part II

Its Children
(Choose 2–3 typical boys and girls from different sections
of this country.  Give them fictitious but typical names, and
make at least one note or sentence about them for each part
of the following questionnaire, or simply write a brief
descriptive paragraph about each child, including the same
kind of information.

Children of _____

|  | Child 1 | Child 2 | Child 3 |
|---|---|---|---|
| Name |  |  |  |
| Sex |  |  |  |
| Home |  |  |  |
| School |  |  |  |
| Playtime |  |  |  |
| Clothing |  |  |  |
| Parents' Occupations |  |  |  |
| Something Special |  |  |  |

Part III    Its History

A.  Who were the early settlers here?

_____

_____

B.  Where did they come from?

_____

_____

_____

C.  How did they live?

_____

_____

_____

D.  Was this country at one time owned or governed by another
country? _____
Name the "mother" country. _____

E.  Is this country now independent (does it have its own
government?)? _____
If so, how did this come to happen?

_____

_____

_____

_____

_____

F.  List any significant facts, events, or people's names
    which should be remembered as historically important
    in the development of the country and tell <u>why</u> they are
    important.

Important Facts, Events, Names | Significance
--- | ---
_____ | _____
_____ | _____
_____ | _____
_____ | _____
_____ | _____

Part IV    Its Daily Life

A.    What kind of government controls the country?

_____

_____

_____

B.    What special ethnic, social, or cultural groups of people
      make up this country's population?

_____

_____

_____

_____

C.    What are the major occupations of the working people?

_____

_____

D. Describe briefly:

Present Transportation Systems: _____

_____

_____

Present Communication Systems: . _____

_____

_____

E. List the country's major natural resources:

_____

_____

Part V    Its Pride and Treasures
List the special people, places, events, possessions of which
this country is especially proud.  Choose one of them on which
to prepare a special presentation for the class.  You choose
the media!!  Make it very exciting for your classmates to
observe or listen to!!

| People | Places | Events | Other |
|--------|--------|--------|-------|
|        |        |        |       |

Part VI    Find a story, poem, song, game, or picture of an art treasure
which has been composed in or about this country.  Share it with
the class.

# FINDING OUT ABOUT A STATE OR PROVINCE
## (Outline for studying a state or province)

Name _____

Name of State or Province _____

I    <u>The Lay of the Land</u>

In the space below draw or paste a map that shows where the state or province is located.

On the lines provided write some words or sentences that tell what the land is like in this place.

Words That Describe the Land:

_____

_____

_____

II   Looking Back

   A.   Who were the earliest settlers here?

   _____

   _____

   B.   Where did they come from?

   _____

   _____

   _____

   C.   How did they make rules or laws for themselves (govern themselves) in the early days?

   _____

   _____

   _____

   _____

   D.   List at least 3-5 significant events that contributed to the development of this new state or province.

   _____

   _____

   _____

   _____

   _____

III   A Look At This Place Today

   A.   A list of the major cities:

   _____      _____

   _____      _____

   _____      _____

B. A list of the major occupations by which the people earn a living:

_____

_____

_____

C. What things does this particular state or province <u>do</u> or <u>produce</u> to contribute to other parts of the nation?

_____

_____

_____

_____

D. A list of the most important natural resources:

_____

_____

_____

_____

E. Some special annual events or celebrations that take place here are:

_____

_____

_____

_____

_____

IV    Shaking the Family Tree

Find out about at least three interesting, creative, or inventive
people who were born or raised here or have lived in this state
or province.  Use the following "PROUD" poster to name and
record information about these people.  (Be sure to choose persons
of both sexes!)

V    More Prides and Treasures

Use a large sheet of construction paper to create an advertisement
for special places of beauty, entertainment, or historical
importance that might be visited in this state or province.  Choose
places you and your classmates might enjoy seeing.  Try to
include drawings or pictures of some of the places on your
advertisement.

VI   From My Point of View

Use the following space to make notes of facts and interesting
things about this state or province that have especially intrigued
you.  (You might note the state bird, flower, or song; songs and
literature written about or in this place; the congress people who
represent this territory in national government; special resorts
and vacation places you have visited or would like to visit, etc.)

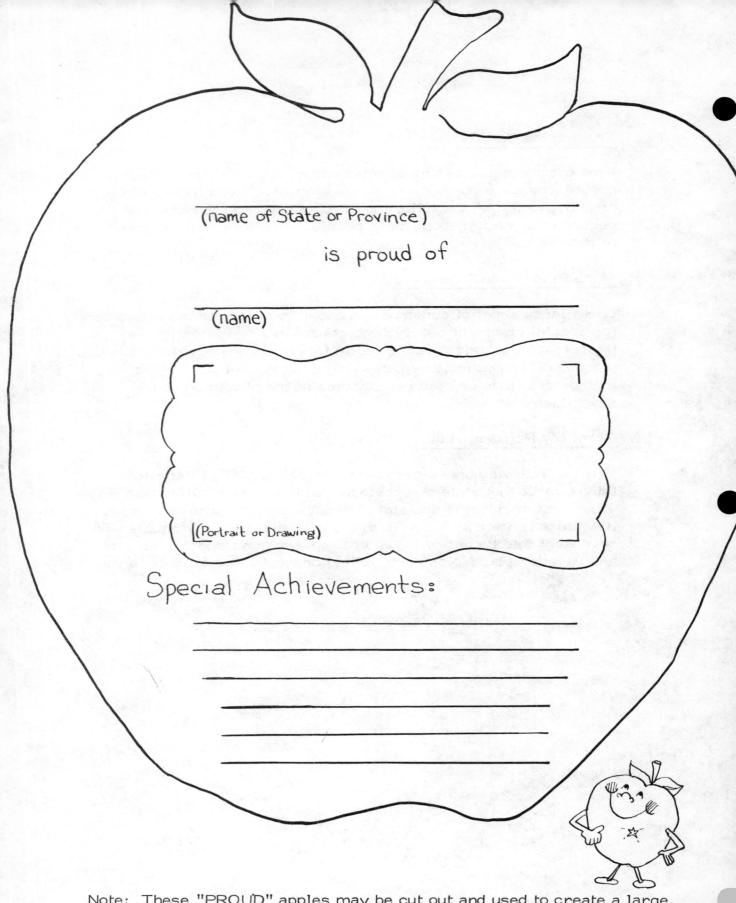

_____

(name of State or Province)

is proud of

_____

(name)

(Portrait or Drawing)

Special Achievements:

_____
_____
_____
_____
_____

Note: These "PROUD" apples may be cut out and used to create a large, bulletin board-size family tree of favorite sons and daughters from the states or provinces.

296

# SOCIAL STUDIES CHECK LIST

_____      _____
          Child's Name                              Birthdate

_____

I.        Understanding of Self

     _____   exhibits awareness of self as a member of a family

     _____   exhibits awareness of self as a member of a peer group

     _____   exhibits awareness of self as a unique human being

     _____   exhibits awareness of the need to become independent in thought and action

     _____   accepts authority

     _____   defends own rights and individuality

     _____   exhibits awareness of self as a free responsible citizen

     _____   exhibits concern for own health and safety

II.      Understanding of the Social Environment

     _____   accepts and respects the worth and rights of others

     _____   exhibits concern for the health and safety of others

     _____   practices courtesy

     _____   exhibits awareness of human interdependence

     _____   exhibits respect for common or public property

     _____   regards rules and laws as necessary for helping people live together peacefully and comfortably

III.   Understanding of the Physical Environment

     _____   exhibits understanding of the size, shape, and motion of the earth

     _____   is oriented to location in relation to objects in the environment

_____ expresses distance and size in relative terms (nearer, farther, bigger, smaller)

_____ exhibits understanding of the relativity of scale to reality

_____ interprets symbols in maps and globes

IV. Understanding of the Economic Environment

_____ understands that people do many kinds of work to earn a living

_____ is aware of the central role of price in a money economy

_____ is aware of the process of converting resources into goods and services to satisfy human wants

_____ is aware of the economic factor of scarcity and the need for economizing resources

V. Understanding of the Historical Past

_____ exhibits understanding that many generations of life have preceded this time in history

_____ exhibits awareness of time measurements and the significance of change which has taken place through time

_____ exhibits respect for cultural customs and traditions of the past

VI. Understanding of the Implications of the Future

_____ understands that change is inevitable

_____ exhibits awareness of personal responsibility for positive change

_____ exhibits openness to new ideas and willingness to expand horizon

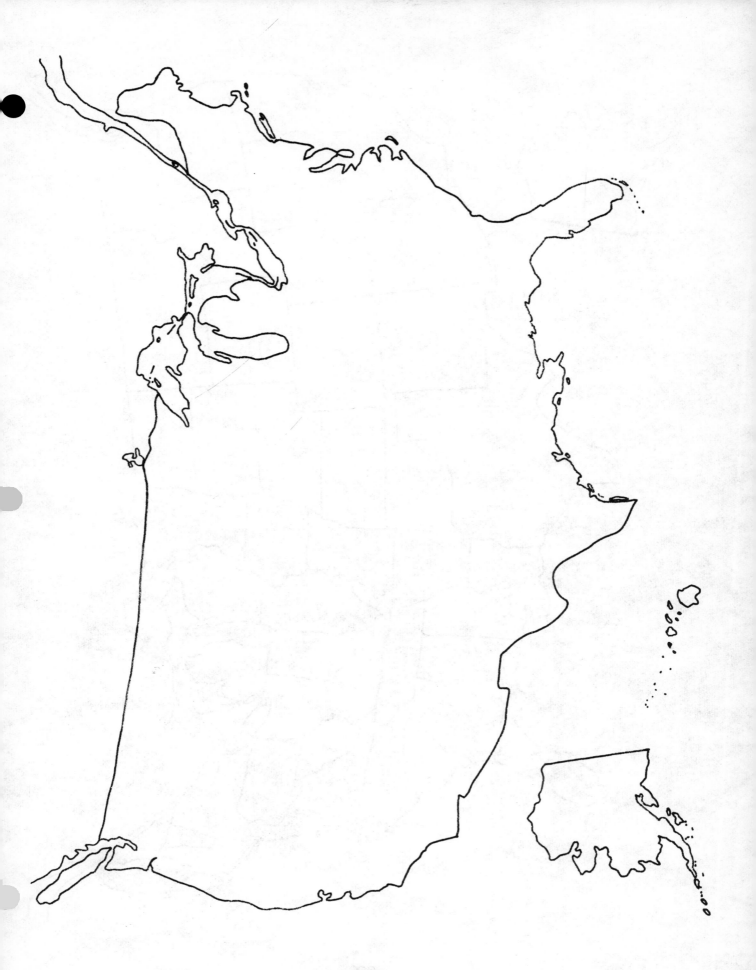

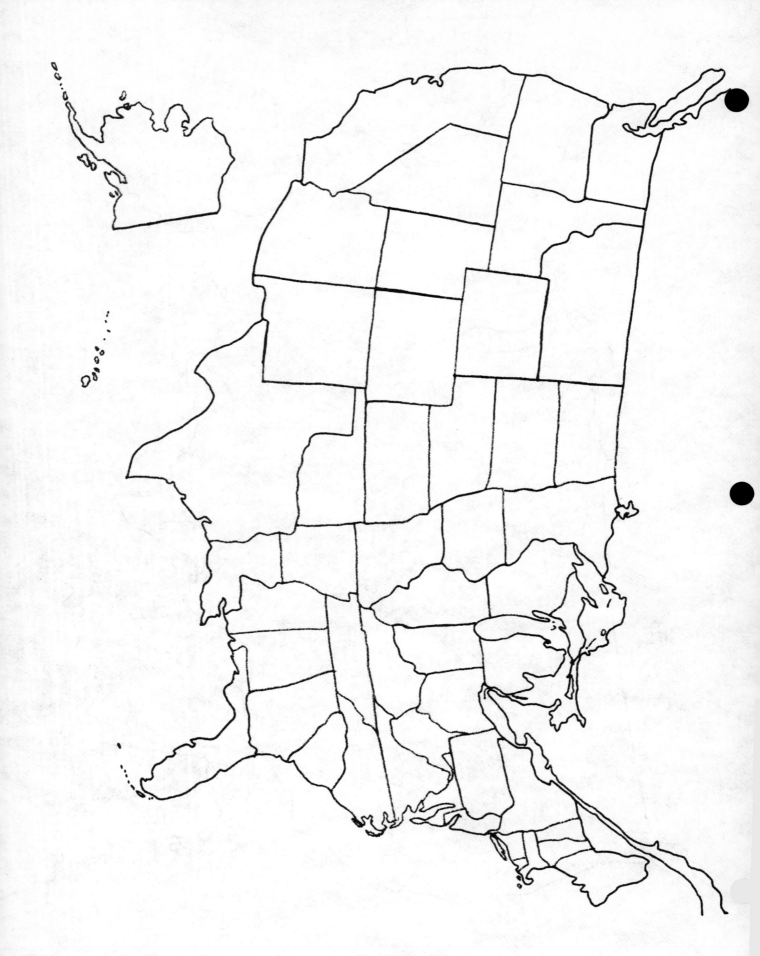

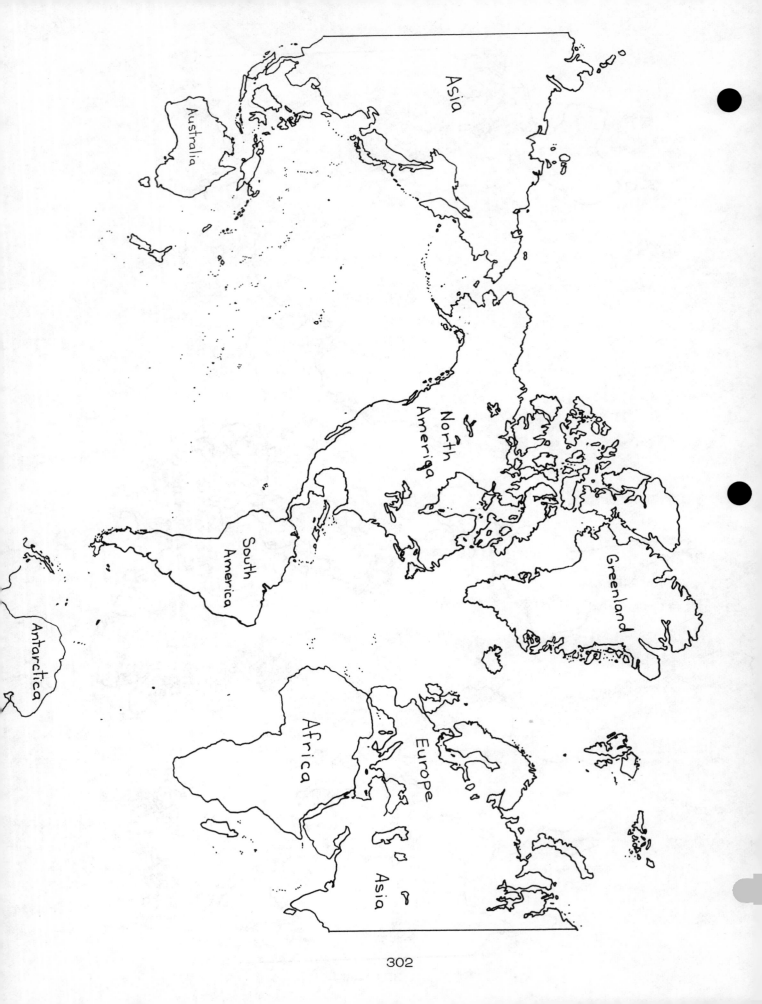

# SELECTED STUDENT REFERENCES

Adamson, Joy. Born Free. New York: Pantheon Books, 1960.

Animals in Danger. Chicago: Field Enterprises Educational Corporation, 1974.

Applegarth, Margaret T. Heirlooms. New York: Harper & Row, Publishers, 1967.

Asimov, Isaac. ABC's of Space. New York: Walker & Co., 1969.

Barr, Jene. What Can Money Do? Chicago: Albert Whitman & Co., 1967.

Bartlett, Margaret Farrington. The Clean Brook. New York: Thomas Y. Crowell Co., 1960.

_____. Where the Brook Begins. New York: Thomas Y. Crowell Co., 1961.

Baylor, Byrd. Before You Came This Way. New York: E. P. Dutton & Co., 1969.

Bendick, Jeanne. The First Book of Ships. New York: Franklin Watts, 1959.

Benziger, Barbara. Controlling Your Weight. New York: Franklin Watts, 1973.

Berger, Gilda. Jobs That Help the Consumer and Homemaker. New York: Lothrop, Lee & Shepard, 1974.

Berger, Melvin. Consumer Protection Labs. New York: John Day Co., 1975.

Bielawski, Joseph G. My Country, U.S.A. New York: Golden Press, 1967.

Botkin, Ben and Withers, Carl. The Illustrated Book of American Folklore. New York: Grosset & Dunlap, 1958.

Campbell, Ann. Let's Find Out About Boats. New York: Franklin Watts, 1967.

Carlisle, Norman and Carlisle, Madelyn. The True Book of Bridges. Chicago: Children's Press, 1965.

Carmer, Carl. Pets at the White House. New York: E. P. Dutton & Co., 1962.

Carpenter, Allan. Chile. Chicago: Children's Press, 1969.

Carpenter, Allan. _New Hampshire_. Chicago: Children's Press, 1967.

Carpenter, Allan. _Vermont_. Chicago: Children's Press, 1967.

Carpenter, Allen and Barlow, Tom. _Guyana_. Chicago: Children's Press, 1970.

Chernoff, Goldie Taub. _Just A Box?_ New York: Walker & Co., 1973.

Chester, Michael. _Let's Go to the Moon_. New York: G. P. Putnam's Sons, 1974.

Cram, George F. _Atlas of the World_. Indianapolis: George F. Cram Co., 1975.

Daugherty, Sonia. _Ten Brave Women_. Philadelphia: J. B. Lippincott Co., 1953.

Doherty, C. H. _Bridges_. New York: Meredith Press, 1969.

Elkin, Benjamin. _The True Book of Money_. Chicago: Children's Press, 1960.

Elting, Mary and Folsom, Franklin. _The Answer Book of History_. New York: Grosset & Dunlap, 1966.

Giovanni, Nikki. _Ego-Tripping_. Westport, New York: Lawrence Hill & Co., 1973.

Graham, Ada and Graham, Frank, Jr. _The Great American Shopping Cart_. New York: Simon & Schuster, 1969.

Green, M. C. and Targett, B. R. H. _Space Age Puppets and Masks_. Boston: Boston Plays, 1969.

Harbin, E. O. _Games for Boys and Girls_. New York: Abingdon Press, 1951.

Holland, Janice. _They Built A City_. New York: Charles Scribner's Sons, 1953.

Hopkins, Lee Bennett, comp. _Take Hold!_ New York: Thomas Nelson, 1974.

Hughes, Langston. _Famous Negro Heroes of America_. New York: Dodd, Mead & Co., 1958.

Icenhower, J. B.  The First Book of the Antarctic.  New York: Franklin Watts, 1956.

Jacobs, Leland B., ed.  Poetry for Space Enthusiasts.  Champaign, Ill.: Garrard Publishing Co., 1971.

Kahn, Bernice.  The Organic Living Book.  New York: Viking Press, 1972.

Kherdian, David, ed.  Visions of America.  New York: Macmillan Co., 1973.

Klein, H. Arthur.  Oceans and Continents in Motion.  Philadelphia: J. B. Lippincott Co., 1972.

Knight, David C.  From Log Roller to Lunar Rover.  New York: Parents Magazine Press, 1974.

Lauber, Patricia.  The Look-It-Up Book of the 50 States.  New York: Random House, 1967.

Laycock, George.  Autumn of the Eagle.  New York: Charles Scribner's Sons, 1973.

Leaf, Munro.  Who Cares? I Do.  New York: J. B. Lippincott Co., 1971.

Liberty, Gene.  The First Book of Tools.  New York: Franklin Watts, 1960.

Lobsenz, Norman.  The First Book of National Monuments.  New York: Franklin Watts, 1959.

_____.  The First Book of National Parks.  New York: Franklin Watts, 1959.

Margolis, Richard J.  Looking for a Place.  Philadelphia: J. B. Lippincott Co., 1969.

Mendoza, George.  The World From My Window.  New York: Hawthorn Books, 1969.

Milgrom, Harry.  ABC of Ecology.  New York: Macmillan Co., 1972.

Millen, Nina.  Children's Games From Many Lands.  New York: Friendship Press, 1965.

Moore, Patrick.  Exploring the World.  New York: Franklin Watts, 1966.

Morse, Doug.  The Brook Book.  Newburyport, Mass.: Storyfold, 1975.

McLeod, Sterling. Careers in Consumer Protection. New York: Julian
    Messner, 1974.

Nathan, Dorothy. Women of Courage. New York: Random House, 1964.

Neal, Harry Edward. The Protectors. New York: Julian Messner, 1968.

Oppenheim, Joanne. Have You Seen Roads? Reading, Mass.: Young Scott
    Books, 1969.

Pitt, Valerie. Let's Find Out About the Red Cross. New York: Franklin
    Watts, 1969.

Podendorf, Ella. Every Day Is Earth Day. Chicago: Children's Press, 1971.

Powell, Meredith and Yokubinas, Gail. What to Be? Chicago: Children's
    Press, 1972.

Pringle, Lawrence. The Only Earth We Have. New York: Macmillan Co., 196

Prochnow, Herbert V. and Prochnow, Herbert V., Jr., comps. A Treasury
    of Humorous Quotations. New York: Harper & Row, Publishers, 1969.

Rathkopf, Carol Z. The Red Cross. New York: Franklin Watts, 1971.

Robe, Rosebud Yellow. An Album of the American Indian. New York: Franklin
    Watts, 1969.

Simon, Noel and Geroudet, Paul. Last Survivors. New York: World
    Publishing Co., 1970.

Szasz, Suzanne and Lyman, Susan E. Young Folks' New York. New York:
    Crown Publishers, 1968.

Taylor, Duncan and Cochrane, Louise. The World of Nations. Racine, Wisc.:
    Whitman Publishing Co., 1965.

Turner, James S. The Chemical Feast. New York: Grossman Publishers, 19

Untermeyer, Louis, sel. The Golden Treasury of Poetry. New York: Golden
    Press, 1959.

_____. The World's Greatest Stories. New York: M. Evans
    & Co., 1964.

306

Ward, Ralph T. Steamboats. Indianapolis: Bobbs—Merrill Co., 1973.

Wiesenthal, Eleanor and Wiesenthal, Ted. Let's Find Out About Tools.
    New York: Franklin Watts, 1969.

Wilcox, Louise K. and Burks, Gordon E. What Is Money? Austin, Texas:
    Steck Co., 1959.

Zaffo, George J. The Giant Book of Things in Space. Garden City, New York:
    Doubleday & Co., 1969.

# SELECTED TEACHER REFERENCES

Banks, James A. _Teaching Strategies for Ethnic Studies_. Boston: Allyn & Bacon, 1975.

Berger, Evelyn and Winters, Bonnie A. _Social Studies In the Open Classroom_. New York: Teachers College Press, 1973.

Casteel, Doyle and Stahl, Robert. _Value Clarification In the Classroom_. Pacific Palisades, Calif.: Goodyear Publishing Co., 1975.

Chase, Larry. _The Other Side of the Report Card_. Pacific Palisades, Calif.: Goodyear Publishing Co., 1975.

Farallones. _Making Places, Changing Spaces in School, at Home and Within Ourselves_. New York: Random House, 1971.

Forte, Imogene, Pangle, Mary Ann and Tupa, Robbie. _Pumpkins, Pinwheels & Peppermint Packages - Teacher Edition_. Nashville, Tenn.: Incentive Publications, 1974.

Forte, Imogene and MacKenzie, Joy. _Nooks, Crannies and Corners_. Nashville, Tenn.: Incentive Publications, 1972.

Forte, Imogene and Pangle, Mary Ann. _More Center Stuff for Nooks, Crannies and Corners_. Nashville, Tenn.: Incentive Publications, 1976.

Fraenkel, Jack R. _Helping Students Think and Value_. Englewood Cliffs, N. J.: Prentice-Hall, 1973.

Greer, Mary and Rubinstein, Bonnie. _Will The Real Teacher Please Stand Up?_ Pacific Palisades, Calif.: Goodyear Publishing Co., 1972.

Gross, Richard E., McPhie, Walter E. and Fraenke, Jack R. _Teaching the Social Studies_. Scranton, Pa.: International Textbook Co., 1969.

Jarolimek, John and Foster, Clifford D. _Teaching & Learning in the Elementary School_. New York: Macmillan Co., 1976.

Kaplan, Sandra Nina, Kaplan, Jo Ann Butom, Madsen, Sheila Kunishima, and Gould, Bette Taylor. _A Young Child Experiences_. Pacific Palisades, Calif.: Goodyear Publishing Co., 1975.

Lundsteen, Sara W. _Children Learn to Communicate_. Englewood Cliffs, N. J.: Prentice-Hall, 1976.

Lowenfeld, Viktor and Brittain, W. Lambert. _Creative and Mental Growth_. 6th ed. New York: Macmillan Co., 1975.

Michaelis, John U. and Keach, Everett, Jr.  Teaching Strategies for
Elementary School Social Studies. Itasca, Ill.: F. E. Peacock
Publishers, 1972.

Purkey, William W.  Self Concept and School Achievement.  Englewood
Cliffs, N. J.: Prentice-Hall, 1970.

Raths, Louis E.  Meeting the Needs of Children.  Columbus, Ohio:
Charles E. Merrill Publishing Co., 1972.

Romey, William D.  Risk – Trust – Love:  Learning in a Humane
Environment.  Columbus, Ohio:  Charles E. Merrill Publishing Co.,
1972.

Simon, Sidney B., Holse, Leland W. and Kirschenbaum, Howard.
Values Clarification.  New York:  Hart Publishing Co., 1972.

Simon, Sidney B., Hawley, Robert C. and Britton, David D.  Composition
for Personal Growth.  New York:  Hart Publishing Co., 1973.

Smith, James A.  Creative Teaching of the Social Studies in the Elementary
School.  Boston:  Allyn & Bacon, 1967.

Social Studies Curriculum Materials Data Book.  Boulder, Colorado:
Social Science Educational Consortium, 1971.

Weinland, Thomas P. and Protheroe, Donald W.  Social Science Projects
You Can Do.  Englewood Cliffs, N. J.: Prentice-Hall, 1973.

Youngers, John C. and Aceti, John F.  Simulation Games & Activities for
Social Studies.  Dansville, N. Y.: Instructor Publications, 1974.

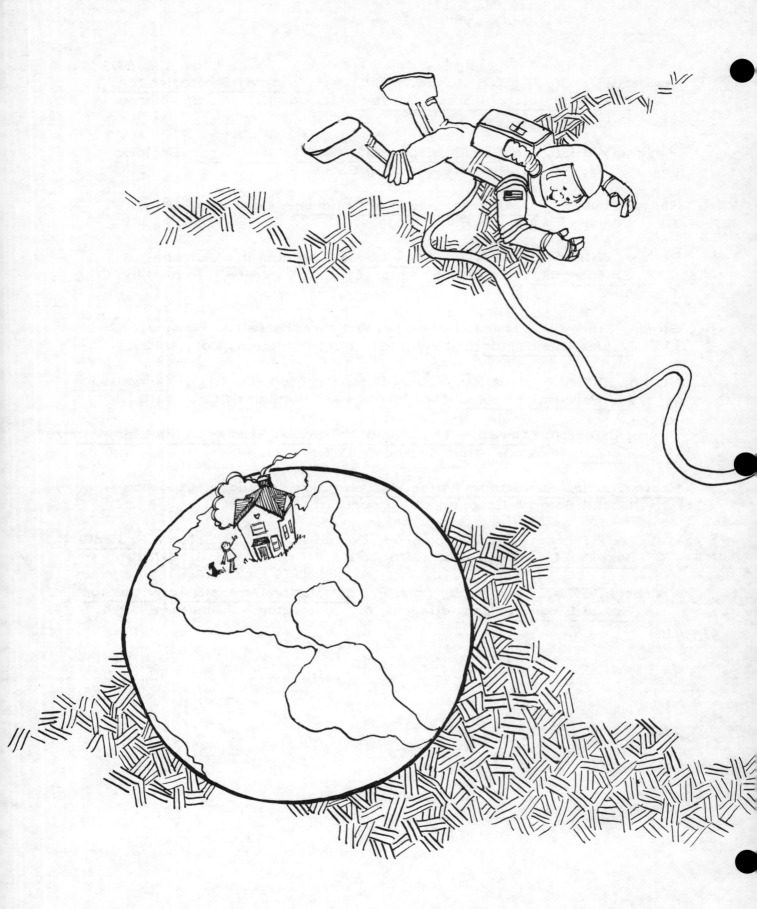

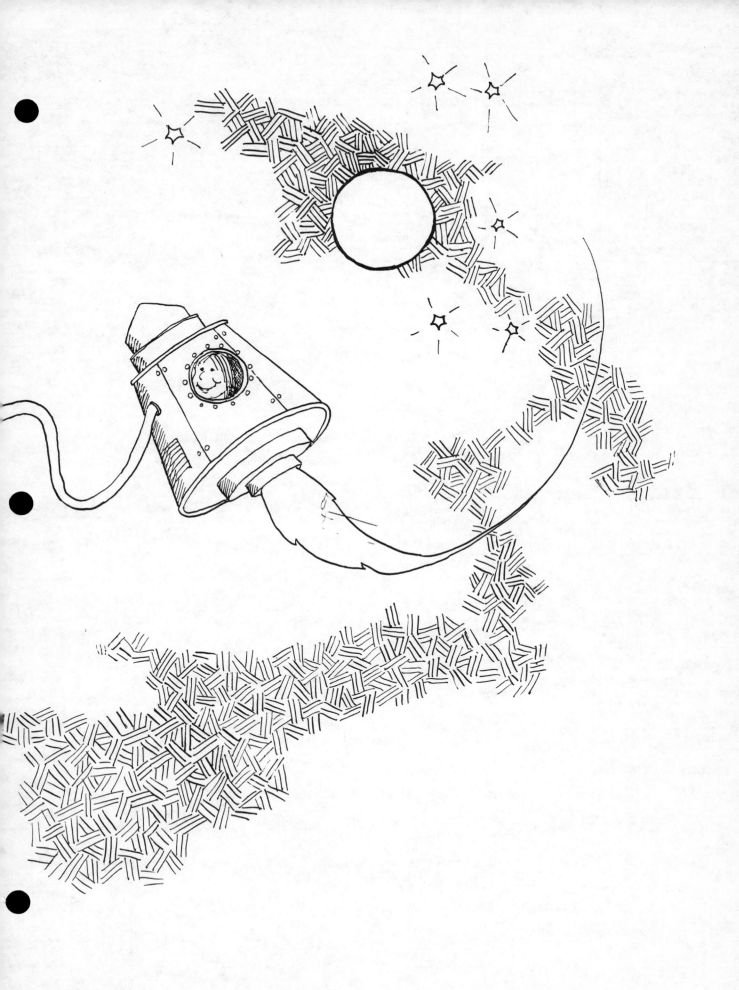